HOW TO Skimm YOUR LIFE

theSkimm®

Ballantine Books

New York

HOW TO Skimm YOUR LIFE

theSkimm®

CONTENTS

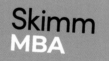

Skimm LIFE · Spilled red wine · Got 8 hours of sleep · Skimm MBA · Got a new job · Negotiated salary

Skimm MBA

Convinced all friends to · an email

Debit card declined while buying muffin

Spit out coffee looking at savings

Stuck to monthly budget

Paid off student loans

Contributed to IRA

Skimm MONEY

Accidentally replied all

Nailed a presentation

Followed the 50-30-20 rule

Skimm Money

Bought a house

Bought a car

Didn't cry looking at account

Skimm THE WORLD

Called a representative

...ted in ...primary

Skimm the World

Skimm'tionary

INTRO

We started theSkimm's adventure seven years ago. We had a lot of ambition, dwindling savings accounts, and two laptops that wouldn't hold a charge. As we grew the business through the years, we often found ourselves asking, "Did everyone else take a class on how to do life? Did I miss that day?"

This book's journey really began four years ago. We didn't know what to read one Memorial Day weekend, and we decided that our Skimm'rs could probably relate. So we started a section in the *Daily Skimm* email newsletter called "Skimm Reads," where we recommended a book we thought our audience might want to have for the long weekend. Our audience liked it, so we recommended another one the next week. And it caught on.

For a few years now, we've been approached about creating a print version of what theSkimm does every day. But start-up rule number one is focus, so we never felt like the timing was quite right.

Now, we're focusing on the next chapter of theSkimm's story. See what we did there?

theSkimm is a **membership for living smarter.** Already a trusted resource for news, we're ready to take on more. We want to help you navigate the noteworthy moments in your *lives,* not just in your days. We want to take all of the daunting, cumbersome, and, frankly, unsexy parts of being an adult, and break them down the same way we break down a complicated news story.

Meet *How to Skimm Your Life.*

This book is the embodiment of our mission, and covers it all: personal finance, career, stress management, global politics, civic engagement, and more.

We built *How to Skimm Your Life* for you. It is our sincere hope that when you close the back cover, you will feel empowered to make a decision or take an action you might not have before. That you feel like you don't need to second-guess yourself, call your parents, phone a friend, or put the decision off until tomorrow.

We hope that you use it as a reference tool, and turn to it time and time again as you navigate the big moments in your life.

We hope it becomes a fixture on your coffee table or on your desk (or even by your couch).

We hope that you share it with a friend. You never know when you'll end up starting a business together . . .

This book has been a dream of ours, and of our team's, for a long time. We can't thank you enough for your support, and we're so excited to share this with you.

Happy Skimm'ng,

Carly & Danielle

Skimm
LIFE

A lot of people say "having it all" is a thing. It's not (except in relation to a buffet). But there are ways to make it easier to manage it all.

"Skimm Life" covers things that will help you stay on top of your life outside work. That includes sleeping, feeling balanced, drinking a glass of wine to unwind, getting OOO, and more.

Things That Make You
Feel Fancy

theSkimm on Wine and Food

Wine is good.

Wine is grape. And de-stressing with a glass is a pastime we recommend. But you probably don't speak sommelier (unless you actually are one. Hi, somm). It's hard to go from "I'll take the second least expensive bottle, thx" to knowing WTF you actually like. Things get even more complicated when you try to play matchmaker. Which foods go well with this vino? Will I ruin my fish with a heavy red? Am I actually partial to the softer California grape? So many questions. So many answers to pour out.

How is wine made?

With a lot of TLC. Wine is basically fermented grape juice. Grapes are de-stemmed and crushed. Then yeast does its part. Yeast is a fungus (stick with us) that can convert sugar into alcohol. This is called **fermentation.** Yeast ferments the grapes; then this juice is aged to soften the taste and bring out more complex flavors.

How should I taste my wine?

With rosé-colored glasses. And slowly. Here are a few steps you should take when sipping your vino.

For when you're figuring out where to start . . .

Color yourself ready. First, check out the wine's color. The color of a wine comes from contact with the grape skins after the grapes have been juiced. The longer the wine's in contact with the skins, the richer the taste and the deeper the color. Brings new meaning to "skin in the game." So its color will give you clues to its taste.

For when you're wondering which glass to use . . .

If you're tasting red wine, you'll have a glass with a wider mouth. Since the flavors are bolder it needs more space to let those aromas mingle and come out to play.

For when you want to look the part . . .

You go swirl. Swirl the wine around in its glass. No, this isn't just to look pretentious, although that's a potential side effect. It's to get more oxygen into the wine. Oxygen is like wine's therapist—it helps it open up and show its true characteristics.

For when it's time to taste . . .

Resist big gulps. The pinkies-out way to taste wine is to let it aspirate. Here's how it works: Roll a sip of wine over your tongue and then suck on it as if you're sucking through a straw. This lets oxygen into the wine and brings out its flavors more. Warning: It may make you look like a fish.

For when you're hot then you're cold . . .

The temp of your wine should depend on what's in your glass.

Thing to know
Paper towel trick. If your wine's too warm, wrap a wet paper towel around it and stick it in the freezer for a few minutes. Ready, set, instant crisp.

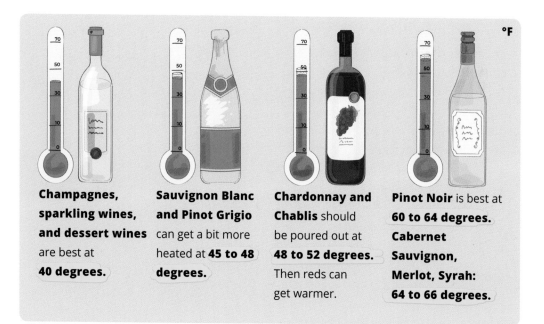

°F

Champagnes, sparkling wines, and dessert wines are best at **40 degrees.**

Sauvignon Blanc and Pinot Grigio can get a bit more heated at **45 to 48 degrees.**

Chardonnay and Chablis should be poured out at **48 to 52 degrees.** Then reds can get warmer.

Pinot Noir is best at **60 to 64 degrees. Cabernet Sauvignon, Merlot, Syrah: 64 to 66 degrees.**

So remember: Bubbly is the most chilled, and the darker the wine the warmer it can get. Red hot.

How do I characterize my wine?

There are a few different categories you should know when talking about the wine in your glass. These include *body, tannins, acidity, oak,* and *variety.*

Talking body

Body refers to the way a wine feels in your mouth. This is in direct relation to how much alcohol is in a wine. A light-bodied wine (think: Riesling) is less than 12.5 percent alcohol and will taste light and crisp. A medium-bodied wine (think: rosé) is between 12.5 and 13.5 percent and will have a *liiittle* more oomph. And a full-bodied or heavy wine (think: Cabernet, Merlot, Malbec) is over 13.5 percent alcohol and will feel more complex and full. It will also make you feel tipsy a little faster, but you'll probably drink it more slowly. Because full-bodied.

Are you tannin or are you out?

You've heard the word **tannin.** You might know what it means, or you might pretend to know. No judgment. Tannins are compounds found inside grape skins, seeds, and stems. They're released when the grape skins, seeds, and stems take a dip in the grape juice post-press. So a wine that's soaked with those things longer will be more tannic. Red wines are higher in tannins than whites. They leave your mouth feeling dry and kinda like you just had dark chocolate or black tea. Many winemakers like tannins because they work as a natural antioxidant to protect the wine. This is a big reason why red wine ages better than white. And why highly tannic wines like Cabernet Sauvignon develop like Jane Fonda: Better. Every. Year.

Kool-Aid acidity test

Here we're talking about a wine's **acidity,** aka when life (wine) gives you lemons. Acidity is that citrusy taste that's formal-speak for words like *crisp, brisk, fresh,* or *bright.* Even wines that you don't think of as citrusy, like heavy reds, have *some* acidity. It's what gives a wine its lift. A wine sans acidity tastes flat or flabby. Yes, *flabby* is a way you can describe wine.

Sow your wild oak

An **oaky** wine means a wine was aged in an oak barrel or became oaky through fermentation. Brand-new barrels give off the most oak flavors, while a used barrel lends texture and softens or rounds out the vino.

we work grape together

The variety show

Variety is a noun that refers to the grape used to make the wine (for example, Chardonnay, Syrah, etc.) while **varietal** is an adjective that describes the wine made using grape varieties. So a Merlot varietal wine could be made up of 75 percent Merlot grapes, meaning Merlot is the dominant grape variety.

How do I know when my wine's gone bad?

First clue: You won't want to keep drinking it. Here are a few things to know about wine that's past its prime.

For when your wine is corked . . .

Psst . . . this doesn't mean there are tiny cork pieces floating in it. It also doesn't mean that your wine's simply expired. It usually means your wine's become contaminated with "cork taint." Translation: Cork taint is when the natural fungi in a cork (sorry for using the word *fungi*) interacts with certain chlorides that are used to sanitize corks. So if a winery uses these types of corks, your wine may become **corked.** A corked wine smells like soggy cardboard. Pass.

For when your wine smells like vinegar . . .

This happens when a type of acid in red wine (acetic acid) interacts with oxygen for too long. Your red will look brownish and smell-slash-taste like vinegar. Pour it out, pour it out . . . into the sink.

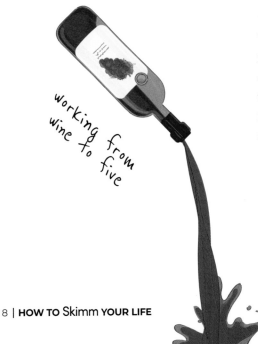

Working from wine to five

For when your wine smells burnt . . .

Surprise, it's **oxidized.** When a wine is exposed to oxygen, it's a good thing at first. But too much of a good thing can make a wine go bad, like a piece of fruit sitting on the counter for too long.

For when you want to know how long your wine keeps after opening it . . .

Sparkling wine

One to three days in the fridge.
Once you pop, the fun does, eventually, stop.

Light white and rosé

Up to a week in the fridge.
Full-bodied white: Three to five days in the fridge.
Full-bodied whites like Chardonnay oxidize faster
because they are exposed to more oxygen in the
winemaking process before bottling.

Red wine

Three to five days in a cool, dark spot.
The more tannins in a red (that is, the darker and
heavier it is) the longer it will keep. So a Cab will keep
for a few days longer than a Pinot Noir.

Before opening wine, it's best to keep it
cool. If it's white, store it in your fridge. If
it's a red, keep it in a cool area of your
house or apartment. And if the wine has a
cork, it's best to store it on its side. It
keeps the wine up against the cork so the
cork doesn't dry out.

How should I shop for wine?

First, read the label. This should include the varietal, region, producer, and alcohol percentage. Sometimes it will shout out the vineyard, estate, reserve, tasting notes, history, or quality level.

For when you can't pronounce anything on the label . . .

That's old news. As in, you're probably dealing with an Old World wine. This may read something like "2009 Château Moulin de Grenet Lussac Saint-Émilion." It's harder to decipher what you'll actually be drinking because the label doesn't mention the wine variety. You have to infer which type of grape comes from the listed region. Enter: Google. In this case, the answer is Merlot.

For when there's a twist top and a colorful label . . .

Got that new new. New World wine labels have both the region and grape variety listed. They might read something like "Cakebread Cellars 2006 Merlot, Napa Valley." This is like the wine that texts you back immediately. You never have to wonder what it really meant.

How should I order wine in a restaurant?

Don't panic if you get a huge list. Check to see if there's a "sommelier's list," which is often made up of the expert's faves, value wines, and unique picks. Also, be wary of ordering a glass vs. a bottle (unless you're solo or really just want one glass). Glasses often have the highest markups, and restaurants don't always store these wines as well. Also be wary of ordering the second cheapest bottle on the menu. A lot of people do this, so restaurants will sometimes put a bottle they're looking to get rid of in that position. You're often better off just going for the cheapest bottle.

How should I pick wine? What should I pair it with?

Spoiler: Some of the rules you think you know (fish needs white; meat needs red) aren't always true. Here's a rundown of how some of the most popular wines taste and what you should pair them with. These go from light to dark.

Sauvignon Blanc

The fruit salad of wines. It's widely planted in France, especially in the Loire Valley. The taste is tart and kind of like an acid party (as in acidity).

Drink it if you like . . .
grapefruit, mint, passion fruit, lemon.

Pair it with . . .
tangy foods—like scallops with grapefruit. The secret's in the sauce. If you have meat in a lemon beurre blanc sauce or light white wine sauce, it will go well with a Sauvignon Blanc. Nutty cheeses like Gruyère are also this wine's PIC.

If you like it, you'll also like . . .
Vermentino (from Italy; more bitter) and Grüner Veltliner (from Austria, with more savory vegetable notes—arugula, turnip, white pepper).

Pinot Grigio

The lemonade stand of wines. This one's the most citrusy of this group and very light. It's planted a lot in Italy. Say *ciao* to a summer day's heavy pour.

Drink it if you like . . .
lemons, limes, pears. Pretty much anything you'd find on a sundress.

Pair it with . . .
salad, flaky fish, light cheeses. Anything a health nut or bird would eat.

If you like it, you'll also like . . .
Albariño (from Spain; more citrusy), Soave (from Italy; more fruity).

Riesling

Raise your hand if you have a sweet tooth. Riesling's known for being sweet, light, and fruity. It's mostly made in Germany and sometimes sipped as a dessert wine. *Das candy.*

Drink it if you like . . .
apples, limes, pears, floral notes.

Pair it when . . .
the spice is right. This one's a good contrast for Chinese and Indian food. If you're drinking it with dessert, a peach cobbler is just . . . peachy.

If you like it, you'll also like . . .
Moscato (from Italy; sweeter).

Chenin Blanc

Bonjour, blanc. This one's from the Loire Valley in France and can vary from dry to sweet.

Drink it if you like . . .
melon, citrus, peach.

Pair it with . . .
sweet and sour. This wine goes well with dishes that have both sweet and sour elements. The most obvious choice: sweet and sour chicken. For the gold star: pork chops with apples.

If you like it, you'll also like . . .
Viognier (drier), Riesling (sweeter).

Chardonnay

Not just your mom's wine. Chards get a rep for being heavy and buttery, but they can't be pigeonholed like that. If they're oaked (aged in an oak barrel) they're fuller bodied with an almost spicy taste. But if they're unoaked (young and wild and free from the barrel) they are zesty and citrus flavored. Chardonn-yay for sticking a cork in the stereotypes.

Drink it if you like . . .
lemon, banana, pineapple (unoaked), or butterscotch, caramel, cinnamon (oaked).

Pair it with . . .
a lot. This goes well with shellfish, chicken, and pork. Also, Brie. Because cheesy is always the way to Brie.

If you like it, you'll also like . . .
Sémillion (lighter), Viognier.

Pinot Noir

Rhymes with *mid-sized car.* It's a medium-bodied red that was first widely planted in France. It leads with higher acidity than most reds and softer tannins.

Drink it if you like . . .
cherry, cranberry, first-impression roses (this smells like one).

Pair it with . . .
pork, chicken, duck, veal. Keeping it veal. Also works with oilier fish like salmon. Opposites attract.

If you like it, you'll also like . . .
Gamay (from the Beaujolais region). It's Pinot Noir's lighter, more floral cousin. Florals, for wine? Groundbreaking.

Merlot

Rhymes with *low.* But it's a high. This is a medium-bodied red that goes down smoothly.

Drink it if you like . . .
plums, cherries, jam. This is your jam.

Pair it with . . .
pasta, lamb, red meat. Can also work with veggie dishes featuring a rich sauce. This one's pretty flexible.

If you like it, you'll also like . . .
Syrah (fuller-bodied), Malbec.

Zinfandel

The wine that works from A to Zinfandel. It's a medium red that's generally high in tannins and alcohol content. It's known for being made in the USA.

Drink it if you like . . .
berry, cherry, spice.

Pair it with . . .
pizza, cheese, grilled cheese. No cheese left behind.

If you like it, you'll also like . . .
Negroamaro (from Italy; same fruity richness).

Syrah

Aka Shiraz. Pronounced *sear-ah*. It's a full-bodied red that's heavily planted in the Rhône Valley in France. *Bonjour*, meaty flavors. Wait for it . . .

Drink it if you like . . .
black pepper, blueberries, meat.

Pair it with . . .
the meat sweats. Sensing a pattern? This will go down well with lamb, smoked meats, etc.

If you like it, you'll also like . . .
Malbec (more chocolate and coffee flavors), Petite Sirah (more tannins and intensity, different from Syrah), Pinotage (South African; more intense/smoky vibes).

Cabernet Sauvignon

The Beyoncé of wines. It's one of the most popular wines in the world, and it originally came from Bordeaux in southwest France, though now it's produced around the whole wine world. It's a full-bodied red and high in tannins.

Drink it if you like . . .
the dark side. Black cherry, cedar, and spice flavors are here.

Pair it with . . .
meats on meats. Lamb, beef, and smoked meats are Cab's friend. You can also get cheesy—firm cheeses like aged cheddar and hard cheeses like Pecorino will taste Gouda with Cab.

If you like it, you'll also like . . .
Merlot (sweeter), Cabernet Franc (higher in acidity), Sangiovese (from Italy; more fruity).

Note: When people say a wine has "hints of cherry," that doesn't mean it's actually made with cherries. It's referring to the flavor of the grapes, which a winemaker can control through how they're grown and pressed.

What about rosé? You forgot rosé!

Just saving the best for last. The final rosé stands alone.

Rosé

The Goldilocks of wine.
It's not too white, not too red, *jusssst* pink. Rosé's made when the skins of the grapes touch the wine for a short period of time. Some think that, like white pants, it's best between Memorial Day and Labor Day. Be a rebel and drink it all year.

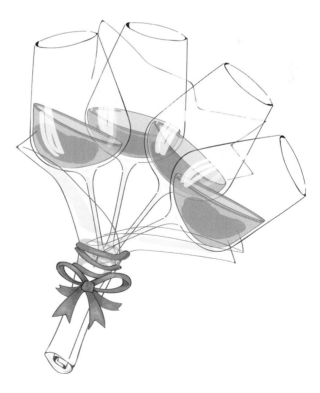

Not to whine (er, wine) but I also want some cocktail halp.

Got your back. Your spirits animal is out there. Yes, spirits. Here are some of Skimm'ologist's favorites and what's in them, so you're never left panic-ordering a vodka soda again.

Moscow Mule

The Best Picture of cocktails.
As in, the glasses are shiny like an Oscar statuette. It's vodka, ginger beer, lime, and a whole lot of kick.

Negroni

The bitter end.
Except it's the beginning. This bitter drink is poured as an aperitif pre-dinner. It's gin, vermouth, Campari, and an orange peel garnish.

Old-Fashioned

The OG.
It's made with bourbon or rye whiskey, sugar, an orange peel, and Angostura bitters (flavored extracts concocted by infusing things like herbs, seeds, and berries with alcohol—aka the every-flavor beans of cocktail ingredients).

Aperol Spritz

The Italian Riviera's arm candy.
This summery favorite is also an aperitif, made up of prosecco, Aperol, and soda. Bon aperitif.

Caipirinha

Brazil's national drink.
It is sugary and tasty. Make it using Brazil's national spirit, *cachaça*, sugar, and lime.

French 75

Bubbly with *le twist*.
It's champagne, gin, lemon juice, and sugar.

Gimlet

Flapper water.
This one's been around since the Jazz Age and includes gin, lime, and simple syrup. Plus a lot of different variations (think: cucumber gimlet). Gim-me gimme.

Paloma

Margarita's (grape) fruity cousin.
It's tequila, grapefruit soda or juice, and lime juice stirred together.

Dark 'n' Stormy

And simple 'n' strong.
Dark rum plus ginger beer.

Pisco Sour

Peruvian special.
Peru's fave liquor, pisco, plus lime, simple syrup, and an egg white. Omelette not included.

Sazerac

The cocktail of New Orleans.
It's rye or brandy, Peychaud's bitters, lemon, and absinthe.

Thing to know
Bitters. Nothing to do with the taste. It's liquor that's intensely flavored with plants and herbs. Think of them like a concentrated shot of flavor for your cocktail.

Brb, tipsy on an empty stomach. Give me something to eat?

As Noah Calhoun said to Allie Hamilton, "What do you want?" When it comes to food, the answer is never simple. This is not a cookbook, although *The Barefoot Skimm'tessa* has a nice ring to it. You're not going to get recipes here. You will get some go-to hacks for convincing people you can kinda cook and stay alive on a budget.

For when that pan you've had since college needs a makeover . . .

Dress your kitchen for the job it wants: to pass as a place where adults live. Here are some pieces of kitchenware you need to whip up something edible. This doesn't include plates and silverware because there's no fun in obvious.

theSkimm's List for Making Your Kitchen Less Sad

Stainless-steel 10-inch skillet
This is HQ for many meals you'll make. Throw in some olive oil and a protein, add some heat, and you've got yourself a Michelin star. ☑

Two cutting boards
One for raw meat, another for produce. Consider making one of them a wood board, since plastic cutting boards can dull your knives. That ain't the sharpest tool in the shed. ☑

Chef's knife
Make it eight to 10 inches. Chop to it. ☑

Measuring spoons and measuring cups
There's a difference between liquid and solid measuring cups—they're specifically designed to measure those types of ingredients, so get both. ☑

Mixing bowl set
For mixing salad dressings, marinades, sauces, and more. ☑

Whisk
Hi, scrambled eggs. And much more. ☑

Locking tongs
A locking mechanism makes it easy to store these. ☑

Slotted spoon
Easy to drain liquid and grease. ☑

Colander
For washing fruits and vegetables, draining canned food, and making a lot of pasta. ☑

add to cart 🛒

For when you're pressed for time and people are coming over...

Say cheese. Can't go wrong with a cheese plate. While we don't discriminate (looking at you, string cheese) there are different types of cheeses you want on your plate.

Fresh and young

Usually made with sheep or goat milk, these are light and white. Includes goat cheese, farmer cheese, and ricotta.

Bloomy rind

Soft and fluffy with a mushroomy or earthy taste and a white rind. Includes Brie and Camembert.

Washed rind

Soft to semi-soft with an orange rind and a "stinky cheese" vibe. Includes Taleggio and Époisses (pronounced *eh-pwahz*).

Semi-firm

Tangy, savory, and, yup, semi-firm in texture. These cheeses keep longer than their softer plate peers. Most can last one to two months in the fridge if the package is unopened and a few weeks if it is. Includes cheddar, Gouda, and Gruyère.

Firm and aged

Savory with an intense flavor, often of hazelnuts or sautéed butter. Mmmm. Includes Pecorino, Manchego, and Parmesan.

For when the oven timer feels like a countdown to the apocalypse, and you're starting to resent Ina Garten . . .

Order takeout.

theSkimm: Drinking wine and cooking food are supposed to be fun. The more you know, the more comfortable you'll be with the list or the whisk. Pour it up. Fry it up. Make sure the glass is always half full and you're fully full.

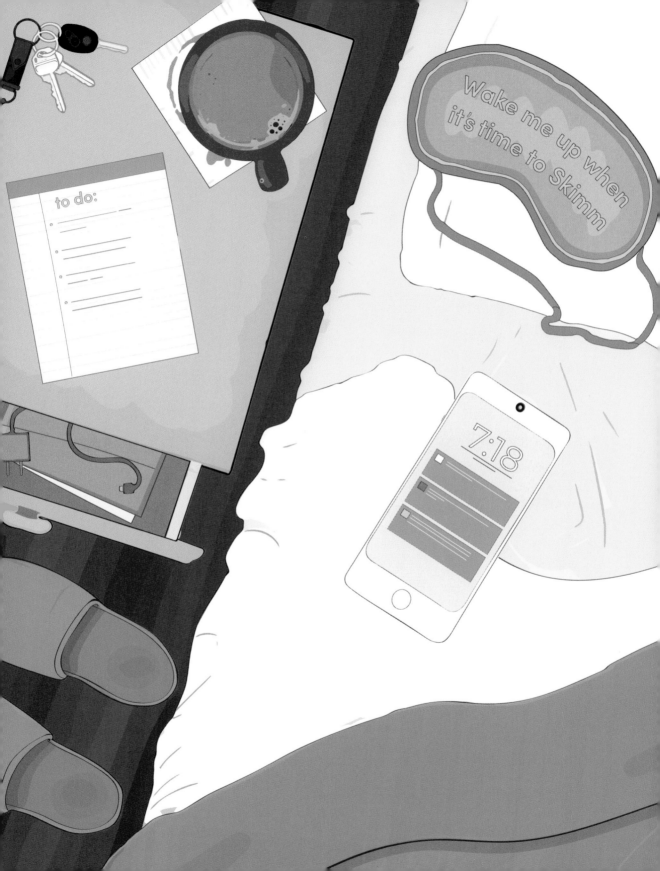

Things That Need a
Deep Breath
theSkimm on De-Stressing

You're busy. Congrats—so is everyone else.

Sometimes it can feel like a competition for who's more overscheduled. This is not a competition you want to win. Insert the de-stress trifecta: sleep, organization, and self-care, aka finding what works for you to stay balanced.

First stop: sleep. It's cliché to use "get more sleep" as a solution to every problem. But clichés are cliché for a reason. Your relationship with your bed is one of the most important ones in your life. It's generous, silent, and doesn't care if you kick it in the middle of the night.

How much sleep should I get?

What's your age again? Use the wisdom of Blink-182 to decide how much *zzz* you need. You probably think eight hours is the golden rule. Turns out, that depends. If you're a newborn, congrats on being a baby genius and reading so early. Also congrats because you're supposed to sleep 12 to 16 hours. Every. Night. Kids who are no longer babies get nine to 11 hours. Adults are supposed to clock in seven to nine hours. Adults over 65 should get seven to eight hours. Then there are those people who say they only need four hours. We say they're lying or they're vampires. PS: Yes, you do need to sleep. Benefits include strengthened memory, higher energy, a faster metabolism . . . and staying awake at work.

What about when I can't get to sleep?

Sometimes sheep don't cut it. It's important to relax the mind before you drift off. People will tell you to meditate before bed and consider taking melatonin. But here are some other, lesser-known tricks that have worked for us.

For the person who has literal sugarplum dreams . . .

Make dinner. In your mind. No, really. Close your eyes and think of the dream meal you'd like to cook, and in your mind, go through all the steps to get that dinner ready. Nothing brings sweet dreams quite like mincing garlic in your head at midnight.

For the person who's soothed by a crossword puzzle . . .

Flip it and reverse it. Aka sing the alphabet backward. Warning: Do not freak out when you get stuck; you are not having a stroke. Warning two: You will soon realize you can get quite good at this, and it will lose its power over time. You can also try counting backward from one hundred.

For the person who thinks history's a snooze . . .

Get schooled. As in, read a long biography. Because there's nothing like a good book about a former president to get your eyelids into gear.

For when you're prone to Instagram rabbit holes . . .

Distance makes the double tap grow fonder. People will tell you to keep your phone in another room. We know you won't do that. So keep it charging on your dresser or somewhere you can't reach, instead of on your bedside table. Or switch your settings to grayscale to make your phone less appealing. Screens (and that includes TVs) are like a traffic jam en route to the Land of Nod.

goodnight moon

For when you have the same thing for breakfast every morning . . .

Make bedtime a habit too. Go to bed and wake up at the same time every PM and AM. Your circadian rhythm (your daily sleep and wake cycle) will stay on track, and you won't feel the need for a post-lunch nap.

goodnight insta

For when you feel all wound up . . .

Just breathe. In through the nose, out through the mouth. Breathing in through the nose helps slow the breath and fight infection, while breathing out through the mouth releases more carbon dioxide. All of which helps you sleep better.

goodnight gmail

For when your head is full of too many things . . .

Take an oxygen break. Use the **4-7-8 breathing technique** to clear your head and relax your mind. Here's how it works: Inhale through your nose for four seconds, hold for seven seconds, and breathe out through your mouth for eight seconds. Another one to try is called **Nadi Shodhana.** It's a yoga breathing technique that's supposed to help you focus. Plug your right nostril and inhale through your left. Then plug your left nostril and exhale through your right. *Aaand* repeat.

For when you want to "live in the moment" . . .

Meet mindfulness meditation. This is the type of meditation that focuses on breathing and bringing your attention to the present moment. The past and the future need not apply. You probably want to start with some help. Check out apps like Headspace and Stop, Breathe & Think for meditation guidance.

How do I avoid pressing snooze?

If you find out, let us know. While the snooze button is unavoidable, here are some wake-up tricks you can keep up your pajama sleeves. You're welcome.

no, seriously, get up

For when you black out . . .

Not like that. Talking blackout curtains. Instead of using them, try cracking your blinds open halfway. When the sun starts rising, the light will suppress melatonin production (aka the hormone that makes you fall asleep) and act like a natural alarm. Cock-a-doodle-snooze.

How should I choose a bed and sheets?

There are some tried-and-true tricks to getting it right. But first, nail down what different terms actually mean.

WTF is a thread count?

Thread count is the thing you're supposed to care about but you might not (yet). It's a sheet's number of horizontal and vertical threads per square inch. Size matters. But bigger isn't always better. Good sheets range anywhere from 200 to 800 thread count. Anything higher is probably BS. Companies can basically use multiple strands of low-quality cotton twisted together to inflate the thread count. So a sheet with 1,000 thread count might actually be worse than one with 400. Translation: Buying anything over 1,000 is like getting SPF 200. Just a marketing tactic.

What about the mattress?

It depends on what kind of sleeper you are. Turns out the way you nod off can help inform which type of mattress you buy.

For when you sleep like a baby . . .

Talking fetal position. This is the most popular *zzz* position. This also applies to **log position,** which is similar to fetal except your legs are straight. People who sleep like this reportedly have the best backs. Fetal and log sleepers should make sure to have a mattress with pressure relief, aka one that disperses their body weight evenly. Memory foam or a softer mattress will do the trick.

For when you sleep stomach down . . .

Cue "Free Fallin'." This position is called the **free fall.** If you sleep like this, you probably want a firm-top mattress so you don't feel like you're being smothered by your bed—memory foam is a stage-five clinger for free-fall sleepers.

For when you throw your hands up in the air . . .

If you're sleeping on your back with your arms out, you're a **starfish** sleeper. You'll want to get the middle child of mattresses—something that's in between. Not too soft, not too hard, *jusssst* right.

What happens between the sheets stays tangled at your feet in the AM. Cue washing. And folding.

Oh, sheet. How *do* I fold a fitted sheet?

1. Turn the other sheet.
First, turn your sheet inside out.

2. Get cornered.
Hold the sheet by the two corners of one of the shorter sides (aka the ones at the foot or head of the bed). Put your hands inside the corners.

3. Prayer-hand emoji.
Bring your right and left hands together. Fold the corner in your right hand over the one in your left, enveloping it. Like the smothering kind of love.

4. Hang low.
Pick up the corner that is hanging in front. Fold it over the two corners in your left hand. The corner that's showing will be inside out.

5. Bring 'em up.
Bring the last corner up, and fold it over the others; it should cover the other three corners.

6. Life is a flat surface.
Lay the folded sheet on a flat surface.

7. It takes two.
Fold the two edges. Make sure the elastic is hidden.

8. Get geometric.
Fold the sheet into a rectangle. Continue folding until the rectangle is the right size so you can fit it in your drawer.

9. Change your name to Martha Stewart.

I got no sleep last night. How do I deal at work?

Make sure to choose a conference room with good pillows. While getting zero sleep is not ideal, there are ways you can try to avoid the midafternoon nap at work.

For when your eyes are going bleary catching up on emails . . .

Get a pick-me-up and do the sole survivor. Here's how it works: Pick your feet up under your desk and hold for as long as you can. This will engage your core and give you an energy boost during the day.

Note: The only real solution for feeling exhausted at work is getting to bed at a reasonable time. And if your space is neat, it'll make you feel more relaxed and ready to unwind. Decluttering and cleaning will also make you more productive and clear-minded.

OK, so how do I keep my space neat?

Put something down. Pick it up. Put it away. Repeat. That's a good start. Then raise your hand if you've ever felt personally victimized by Marie Kondo. The most effective way to reduce clutter is simple: Get rid of sh*t. We know that's easier said than done. Here are some tricks to make your space and life more zen.

For when your closet is overflowing . . .

Apartments and extra baggage do not play well together. Use the **hanger trick** to get rid of or donate the stuff you don't actually wear. Here's how it works: Turn all your hangers one way. After you've worn an item—and only after you've worn it—turn its hanger the other way. After six months, the writing will be on the closet wall.

For when your co-worker's window shopping during a meeting . . .

The "add to cart" addiction is real. Meet the **30-day list.** For 30 days, do not buy anything except necessities. When you want to buy something, write it down in a Google doc, the Notes app, or wherever you keep your to-do list. At the end of 30 days, if you still want the thing on the list, have at it.

For when you have piles on piles in your living room . . .

Take the **12-12-12 challenge.** Find 12 things to throw away, 12 to donate, and 12 to put back in their place.

But what about keeping my stuff clean?

Chances are, some of that stuff on the floor was dirty. Enter: cleaning and laundry. We are not going to tell you how to do your laundry except to say, *do it.* Wash your sheets once every two weeks. Wash your clothes when you sweat in them. Don't be gross.

How do I clean . . .

A shower curtain

How to do it: Put your plastic shower curtain in the laundry machine with some towels, plus half a cup of laundry detergent and half a cup of baking soda. Wash it in warm water on the regular cycle. Then add one cup of white vinegar to the rinse cycle.

How often: You're supposed to do this once a month. But we won't do that, so aim for once every three months.

A toilet

How to do it: You'll need a toilet bowl cleaner, gloves, a toilet brush, and some resolve. Start with the bowl. Put the toilet bowl cleaner around the edge of the bowl and into the bowl and scrub it all with the brush. Add one cup of white vinegar to the toilet after scrubbing and let it sit for an hour. Then flush it away. To clean the outside of the toilet, use the toilet cleaner and a cloth. Work your way from top to bottom.

How often: You're supposed to do this once a week . . . but that seems unrealistic. Start with once a month. No one ever said *Game of Porcelain Thrones* was entertaining.

A makeup brush

How to do it: Get the bristles wet with lukewarm water and rub with a drop of soap. Rinse it off like you'd shampoo your hair. Then let the brush dry on the edge of a counter (avoid putting it on a towel because it can mildew this way). You can also buy wipes for this if you want a shortcut.

How often: You're supposed to wash brushes that are around your eyes twice a month and all others once a month.

A trash can
How to do it: Gloves on again. Yes, you do need to clean your trash can so it doesn't smell. Wash it out with a hose—put it in a bathtub, outside, or somewhere you can hose it down. Spray with a disinfectant cleaner and then scrub it with the toilet brush (it's *baaaack*). Now bring out the hose again and spray it all down.

How often: Do this once a month or whenever you feel like cleaning. Spoiler: It can be surprisingly satisfying.

A refrigerator
How to do it: Take (or eat) the food out of the fridge. Then remove all drawers and shelves and soak them in warm water and dish soap. Get a sponge and wipe down the interior with warm water and dish soap. Baking soda mixed with warm water is your secret weapon to remove leftover stains. Leave it on for a minute and then wipe off.

How often: Once a season.

An AC
How to do it: "No filter" is not a humblebrag here. The filter on your AC is essential to making sure the air in the room is clean. So you need to make sure the filter itself is clean. For a window unit, unplug it and then remove the front plate. Vacuum the coils to get sh*t that blocks air out. Check the drain pan (the part that pulls out) for algae,

y'all know me,
still the same ac

and wash it out with water. Then check the filter and replace it if it looks damaged or dirty. For central AC, wash down the condenser (the part that's outside) with a hose. To clean the inside, unscrew the fan and move it aside. Use that same vacuum hose to clean out the inside. Then remove the air filter and use a narrow vacuum attachment to clean it out.

How often: Once a year.

There are some other things that will throw cleaning curve balls at you . . .

How do I get out a grass stain?

Combine one tablespoon of white vinegar and two tablespoons of water into a solution. Pour it out onto the stain. Let it sit for 15 minutes, then lightly scrub it with a toothbrush. Throw it in the wash and voilà—grass is no longer greener.

Grease stain?

You've got this. Remember: Every pizza is a personal pizza if you believe in yourself. Every pizza grease stain is treatable if you use dish detergent. All you have to do is lightly scrub the detergent into the spot and then wash per usual. Piece of (greasy) pie.

Wine stain?

Get salty. Not talking about your comebacks after a few glasses. Salt is the tried-and-true secret wine stain weapon. First, blot out the wine (whether it's on a shirt or a carpet). Do not rub the stain. Then pour a LOT of salt over the stain and let it dry. Wash with cold water. Some people like to pour club soda over the stain first. For very large or intense vino fails, try combining three tablespoons of hydrogen peroxide with one tablespoon of dishwashing liquid. Pour over the stain and let it lounge for a while.

Pots and pans?

Add two tablespoons of baking soda to your stained pot or pan and scrub with water.

What about my duvet?

You should wash the duvet cover in the washing machine as often as your sheets (at least once every two weeks). And wash the actual duvet once every two to three months, also in the washing machine. But check the label to make sure yours doesn't need to be dry-cleaned.

OK, my stuff is clean-ish. What about my face?

It's a wide skincare world out there. A lot of terms get thrown at (and on) your face. Whether your routine is soap and water or full of products we can't pronounce, it's helpful to know what's available. Here's the 411 on some popular ingredients and products.

Toner

The balancing act. It's a liquid meant to get the skin's pH balance in check. Skin is naturally acidic. But cleansers are more alkaline, which can throw the skin's pH levels off-kilter. Some toners can remove oil and minimize pores, so experts recommend them most for people with oily skin. It's optional, but it should be used right after cleansing.

Serum

A vitamin shot for your face. It's usually a water-based product that goes deep. As in, it's made up of small molecules that can get deep into your skin to deliver good ingredients. That can include vitamin C, one of the most popular types of serums. It's also optional but should be used after toning. You can also apply multiple serums and layer them. Go wild.

Retinol

A form of vitamin A. And it gets an A grade in the anti-aging category. Retinol's meant to reduce fine lines and increase collagen production. It's supposed to be used after cleansing and before moisturizing at night. Less is more—a pea-sized drop is all it takes. Retinols may cause redness and drying at the beginning, so start small and use only once a week. Your skin has to build up a tolerance to it.

Hyaluronic acid

There are multiple "acids" you hear about for your skin (like glycolic acid, which is used for exfoliation). Hyaluronic acid is an ingredient that holds moisture in your face and helps keep skin hydrated. But for most people, it doesn't replace a moisturizer. It helps your skin hold moisture while a traditional moisturizer seals that moisture in. Moisture is the essence of wetness and wetness is the essence of beauty.

My face is clean but my head's still a mess.

Enter: food and exercise. These can help focus your mind and improve your mood. Mental health should always come first. More on that later.

For when you're feeling antsy . . .

Get a move on it. This may seem obvious, but exercise is proven to improve your mood. Because endorphins make you happy. Studies have shown that 30 minutes a day is all you *really* need. 30 minutes: the amount of time you spent stalking your ex's cousin's best friend's dog. If you're not into running, some other types of exercise to try include, yup, yoga (good for relaxation), swimming (good for working out the whole body without putting strain on the joints), or . . . drumroll please . . . walking. Never forget: Power walking is an Olympic sport.

WALKED A BIT

#1 Athlete

I'm too busy to work out.

We see your to-do list and raise you deskercize. Exercising at your desk is the best way to multitask.

For when you get a second wind . . .

I'm so excited! I'm so scared! Keep the '90s nostalgia going with the butterfly clip. Under your desk, alternate lifting each leg up and then tapping each foot to the floor so your legs are fluttering like, yup, a butterfly. Do this until your legs hurt or someone notices.

For when your boss is OOO . . .

This means snack time. As in, get some calorie-free dip. Use your desk chair to do triceps dips. Put your hands at the edge of your chair, bend your elbows, dip it low, bring it up slow.

For when you're feeling sleepy . . .

Remember your friend from earlier, the sole survivor. Lift up your legs for an instant pick-me-up and core exercise.

How often should I go to the doctor?

At minimum, once a year to your primary care provider and OB-GYN. And twice a year to the dentist. And women ages 50 to 75 should get a mammogram every two years to screen for breast cancer, while women 40 to 49 should talk to their doctors about their history to decide how often or if they should get mammograms.

Anything I can eat to feel better?

Chocolate. But seriously, you probably already know which foods are considered healthy vs. not so much. People will tell you to eat grains, fish, a lot of greens, and to bring bags of unsalted almonds on the plane instead of taking the pretzels. We're here to tell you it's OK to take the pretzels. But also to say that there's a reason power foods are called power foods. Here's a list of some and the reasons *why* certain foods give you gold stars in the health category. Plot twist: Most of them actually taste good.

Berries

Berry good for you, since they're high in antioxidants. Antioxidants can act like cell healers. They can repair damaged cells and help you say "bye" to sickness.

Mushrooms

Veg out. Studies show that 'shrooms might help stabilize blood-sugar levels, which can even out your mood. They also promote healthy gut bacteria. And nerve cells in our gut contain most of our body's serotonin (aka a chemical that helps regulate mood).

Avocado

Not just a punch line about millennials. A large percentage of an avocado is made up of healthy fats (specifically something called oleic acid) that help your brain run smoothly.

Tomatoes

Whether it's a tomato or a tomatoe, it contains a nutrient called lycopene. It gives tomatoes their red pigment and some studies have linked it to a healthy heart, protection against certain types of cancers, and even protecting the skin from UV damage.

What about health food ingredients I can't pronounce?

Açaí

Pronounced *ah-sah-ee*. They're berries found on South American palm trees. While some of açaí's benefits haven't been proven, it contains antioxidants and is relatively low in sugar compared to most fruits. But that's the pure berry form. Açaí bowls, on the other hand, can be loaded with sugar.

Chia

Not the pet. These seeds are tiny but pack a big punch. They come from a Central American mint plant and are high in nutrients like omega-3 fatty acids, fiber, and protein. All of which help keep your energy levels up and mind focused.

Flax

Pronounceable and versatile. Flaxseed can be used to make linen . . . or be put in your smoothie. The seeds come from the flax plant, and they're high in those omega-3s and in fiber.

Hemp

We can pronounce this one, but that doesn't make it less trendy. Hemp seeds come from the hemp plant. They're the same species as cannabis but a different variety. Spoiler: They won't get you high. But they are high in fatty acids and protein.

CBD

Stands for cannabidiol. It comes from the flowers or buds of hemp and marijuana plants but it's a different chemical from THC (the one that gets people high). While there are a lot of claims around CBD oil as a magic ingredient, the most significant health benefits include pain relief and epilepsy treatment.

It's not revolutionary to claim "Eat well and exercise" is the recipe for good health. But it goes beyond that too.

theSkimm: Life moves pretty fast. If you don't stop and look around once in a while, you could miss it . . . or get really stressed out.

What about mental health?

If you think you or someone you know has signs or symptoms of a mental health condition, do not self-diagnose. Mental health conditions don't improve on their own, and if untreated, may get worse over time and cause serious problems. Get treatment from a doctor who's trained to help.

How do I find that person?

If you have health insurance: Start on your insurance provider's site. Most healthcare plans in the US offer mental health benefits just like they offer medical or surgical benefits. So if you have insurance, there's a good chance you can get subsidized access to mental health treatments, like therapy.

If you can't find coverage through insurance: Check to see if you can find help through a Federally Qualified Health Center (visit hrsa.gov). Experts also recommend reaching out to the Crisis Text Line by texting 741741, which offers free help all day, every day.

If you or someone you know is struggling with suicidal thoughts, call 1-800-273-8255, the National Suicide Prevention Lifeline.

Reminder: It is illegal for your employer to discriminate against you because of your mental health condition. In many cases, it's on your employer to provide accommodation so you can do your job right (for example, time off for therapy, unpaid leave).

Things Ready for Takeoff

theSkimm on Travel

Time to talk about the triple O.

Not that kind of O. Talking OOO, or Out of Office. Travel is important for recharging, seeing the world, and getting out of your comfort zone. You know this. But taking a trip also comes with a lot of logistics and a lot of question marks.

This chapter will make sure the only baggage you bring with you is literal. Hint: You'll learn how to leave travel issues, overstuffed suitcases, planning problems, and jet lag at home.

How can I skip the lines at the airport?

Few feelings are better than cutting in line. You have a few options. These are listed from least to most expensive.

For the traveler who forgets to wear socks . . .

Keep your shoes on. **TSA PreCheck** is the most popular option to make your trip smoother. It gets you through the line quickly, and you don't have to remove shoes, laptops, liquids, belts, or jackets during security. It's also the cheapest option at $85 for a five-year membership. The catch? Applying isn't easy. You have to submit an application online and then go to an in-person interview at an enrollment center (likely at an airport). Do it on a day you already have a flight so that you don't have to go to the airport randomly. It can then take a few weeks to get approved.

Thing to Know
Your "known traveler number." Once you're approved for TSA PreCheck, make sure to save and use this number when booking flights.

For the traveler racking up passport stamps . . .

The world is your line-cutting oyster. **Global Entry** lets you skip the customs line so you can nurse your jet lag faster once you get home. When you get to customs, you just head to the Global Entry kiosk, scan your passport, give your fingerprints, and fill out a customs declaration onscreen. If you have Global Entry, you also get TSA PreCheck. You'll need to do an in-person interview, and then pay $100 for a five-year membership. Once you're approved, you'll get a Global Entry card in the mail.

For the traveler who wants everything at the tip of her finger . . .

Get in the **CLEAR.** This is the program that scans your fingerprints and eyes to get you through the line faster by avoiding the boarding pass–ID checkpoint. All you have to do is head to the CLEAR kiosk at the airport to sign up, or get it done online before your trip. Unlike the other options, there's no wait for approval. The catch? If you don't have TSA PreCheck, you still have to take off your shoes in the line. It's also the priciest option at $179 a year (about $15 a month). This seems *veryyy* steep but may make sense if you travel a lot. Because time is money. Also to be, yes, clear: If you already have TSA PreCheck and are thinking of getting CLEAR, your TSA PreCheck will carry over too.

How do I get flights for cheap?

This can feel like asking how to sleep with a crying baby next to you on the plane: impossible. But there are some tricks you should always have in your carry-on pocket.

For when you don't like travel surprises . . .

Keep it consistent. Book on the same airline so you can rack up rewards points. You also might be able to pay for a partner flight. For example, you can fly any SkyTeam partner with Delta miles—that includes airlines like Air France, KLM, Korean Air, and more. You can search for award flights on the airline website.

your stop

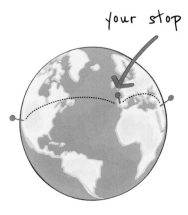

For when you want to turn the weekend into a long weekend . . .

Your wallet says thanks. Because the cheapest days to fly tend to be Tuesdays and Wednesdays. There's also research that says the cheapest day to book is often on Sunday . . . the earlier the better (5 AM is your best bet to find a deal). Have fun with that.

For when you want Kayak to do all the work for you . . .

Might have to do some investigating. Some airlines (cough, Southwest, cough) don't allow comparison sites to use their data. So check airline sites individually before booking to be positive you're scoring the best deal.

OK, I'm all booked up. *Haaalp* me pack.

You probably don't need that fourth pair of shoes but might bring them anyway. Here are some hacks to make the most of your suitcase space.

For when you're having trouble picking favorites . . .

Your clothes are not your children. For a weeklong trip, use the **5-4-3-2-1 rule:**

- ☐ five pairs of socks and underwear
- ☐ four tops
- ☐ three bottoms
- ☐ two pairs of shoes
- ☐ one hat

For when you have to sit on your suitcase to close it . . .

Roll out. Use the **military roll method.** Aka roll your clothes when packing, instead of folding them. You'll be able to get more in your bag, and it reduces wrinkling. Roll underwear and socks, and stuff those inside your shoes to save even more space.

For when your clothes smell musty after being packed . . .

Get your sheet together. Stick a dryer sheet in your suitcase so your clothes come out smelling fresh on the other side.

For when your suitcase is a hot mess during your weekend trips . . .

Be more of a square. Packing cubes can help you fit more into your bag and stay organized once you arrive.

For when your jewelry ends up tangled in your carry-on . . .

Stick a straw in it. There's a trick to fasten your delicate necklaces through paper straws to keep them from getting all knotted. No judgment if you just put yours in a pouch instead.

For when you want to avoid a major shampoo explosion . . .

Paging Ross Geller. Put a piece of plastic wrap in between the bottle opening and the cap. Screw it on tight. It'll look like your cap is wearing a chic skirt.

For when your shoes get dirt on your favorite shirt . . .

Shower your shoes. Put shoes in a shower cap to keep them from spreading sh*t all over your clothes.

But the only thing I *really* want to bring with me is my dog.

Throw your pup a bone and pack him or her as a carry-on. Some airlines will let you fly with a dog under 20 pounds (you'll have to pay around $100 for it, though). If your dog's bigger, you'll need to make him or her an emotional support animal. This is different from a service dog, which is a dog trained to aid someone with a specific disability. An emotional support animal means your pet provides you with therapeutic benefits. If you don't actually qualify for this, you have the option to either check your dog as cargo or leave him or her at home. Distance makes the bark grow louder.

Brb, feeling ruff after so much planning . . .

The best is yet to come. See: jet lag. Jet lag is like the bad ex who always texts you on your birthday: reliable and exhausting. But there are some tricks to ghost it.

For when you're trying to adjust to a new time zone . . .

Clock it in. Make sure to switch to the new time zone once you get on the plane. And prep yourself in the days leading up to your trip. If you're traveling east, go to bed 30 minutes to an hour earlier than usual in the days before your vacay, and wake up 30 minutes earlier than usual. Early to bed, early to press snooze. Flights that get you to your destination in the early evening are also good for catching up on sleep. Then you can *zzz* a few hours after landing. But if you arrive in the AM or middle of the day, try not to nap. It'll throw off your sleep patterns at night. Stay up until your normal bedtime at home and then hit the pillow. Hard.

For when you can't fall asleep on a bumpy plane . . .

Always try to book your seat close to the colonial woman on the wing. The wings are the plane's center of gravity, and sitting near them equals less turbulence and more sleep. And sad news: You're supposed to drink only water on the plane. No wine. Womp womp. That's because both flying and wine drinking can cause dehydration. *Psst* . . . some rules were made to be broken.

I'm going on a trip abroad. What do I need to know?

Aside from the jet lag tips . . . a lot. First up: passport.

For when you need to get a passport . . .

You might think it's basic that we're telling you that you need a passport to go abroad. But raise your hand if you can actually name the steps you take to get one. Bueller?

You need to apply for one at least three months before your trip. If your trip is happening before that, you have to get it expedited. Hi, procrastinator. More on that later, fittingly. Here are the steps you need to take.

Say, what's up, doc?
Doc as in documents. Gather yours. You'll need identification (like a driver's license) photocopied front and back, a proof of US citizenship (a birth certificate or old US passport) photocopied front and back, cash for passport fees, and your application form.

Get in formation.
Fill out the form. Go to the State Department website and fill out a DS-11 form. Print your application, but *do not* sign it.

Take a pic.
Get your passport photo taken. Most post offices will do this for you for an extra fee. If you're doing it on your own, the pic needs to be 2 × 2 inches and printed in color.

Pay up.
It's $35 for the passport acceptance fee and $110 for a new passport book.

If you need your passport within two to three weeks, you should prep the same package as above but be prepared to put some money where your late mouth is. It'll cost $60 to have it expedited.

I have a passport. I just want to renew it.

First things first: Put its expiration date on your calendar. You don't want to be that person who arrives at the airport and finds out her passport expired weeks ago. Note: Many countries require your passport to be valid for six months after your return date. Meaning if your passport's expiring within six months, you won't be able to use it. Your passport's good for 10 years if it was issued when you were 16 or older and for five years if you were 15 or younger. Check yourself before you wreck your trip.

Signed
Print and sign a DS-82 form from the State Department website.

Smize
Take a new passport photo. Reminder: It has to be 2 × 2 inches and sans glasses.

Sealed
Grab your old passport.

Delivered
Mail this whole package to the Passport Processing Center.

What if I lose my passport?

Don't lose your sh*t too. Breathe. Then report it online via the State Department with a DS-64 form. Or, if you'd prefer to speak to a human, call the National Passport Information Center at 1-877-487-2778. They'll likely schedule you to come to the nearest embassy for a passport reissue.

If you lose your passport while you're away . . .

Again, breathe. The embassy can issue you a limited emergency passport that will let you come home to Uncle Sam or continue traveling abroad. Once you're back in the US, you'll have to swap your SOS passport for a perma passport.

How should I tip abroad?

You might not need to. Everywhere has its own tipping practices, so make sure to look yours up before you go.

Here are general restaurant tipping guidelines in some different places . . .

Europe

In the UK and France, restaurants often include a service charge with the bill. If not, it's typical to leave 10–15 percent. In Italy and Spain, 7–10 percent is expected for good service.

Asia

In China and Japan, tipping is actually considered rude in many places. In Thailand, Malaysia, and the Phillipines, 10 percent is generally OK. Many Hong Kong restaurants add a 10–15 percent service charge—if not, leave that much as a tip. In India, tipping isn't required but 10 percent is expected in large cities.

South America

In Argentina, Brazil, Chile, Ecuador, and Peru, 10 percent is usually added at restaurants (if not, tip it). In Colombia, an 8–10 percent tip is often included but it's common to tip more (up to 15–20 percent total).

Africa

In countries including Botswana, Kenya, South Africa, and Morocco, 10 percent is the norm at restaurants if the tip isn't included.

Australia

0–10 percent. Tipping isn't expected but 10 percent at high-end restaurants is a nice addition, mate.

For when you're seeing dollar signs from all the tip money you'll save . . .

Not so fast. Meet sales taxes. The **VAT,** or value-added tax, is the one you should know about. It's an EU thing, and it might as well stand for "very alarming tax." Alarming because it is so confusing. Here's what you should know about it . . .

It was a pleasure serving you!

Tax:	$$.$$
Gratuity:	$$.$$
Service:	$$.$$
Tip:	$$.$$
A little something extra:	$$.$$
Other:	
	$$$.$$

Thanks!

Restroom code: xxxx
Customer Copy

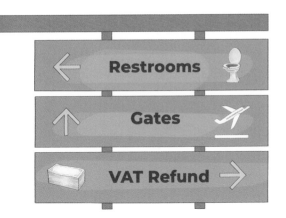

VAT 101

With the VAT, a product is partially taxed at every point of production. As opposed to being taxed only once, like with a national sales tax or state sales tax (which is how the US does it).

The end result of the VAT? A higher tax on stuff you buy.

The trick? You can get a refund for VAT items. When you're shopping, show the merchant your passport and have them fill out a refund document, usually called a "tax-free form." Then bring all of this to customs at the airport you're leaving from. The customs officer may ask you to show them your goods then. So make sure to do this before you check your bag. Then take the certified document to a specific office in the airport or station that processes the paperwork. It can take months to get a refund.

Aaand insert cash back here. If this sounds like a lot of steps, it's because it kinda is. But it makes sense if you're making large purchases.

How should I exchange my money?

If you want cash on hand, head to the bank. Depending on your bank, your debit card can be used at international ATMs to withdraw local currency.

How do I make sure my international data is working?

Get an international package before leaving. And make sure you're not getting down with downloads. Switch off automatic email downloads and background app refreshes. Deactivate automatic syncing to services like iCloud, Google, and Dropbox. If you don't have an international package at all, switch off data roaming to avoid scary charges. In iOS, the toggle switch is under Settings > Cellular. In Android, it's under Settings > Wireless & Networks > Data Usage. Phone calls and texts will come through, but data will be sent and received only when there's Wi-Fi available. So go that route only if you feel Wi-Fine about being MIA for a lot of the trip.

the home is where the wifi connects automatically

This all sounds very expensive.

There are some rules of thumb for how you should budget other expenses in your life (stay tuned), but how much you spend on travel is personal. While you're there, there are some ways to make sure you're saving. One is to go on a **cash diet.** Budget for the amount you want to spend daily and put that amount in different envelopes labeled by day. Just like the days of the week underwear you wore in middle school.

theSkimm: Travel is not always straightforward. But if you do it right, you'll stay fly . . . and have the pictures and refreshed mind-set to prove it.

Things Mother Nature Likes
theSkimm on Going Green

It's not easy being green . . . but it's easier than you think.

If you're worried about being judged for your bad habits, you're not alone. But it's worth becoming more environmentally friendly one step at a time, and it doesn't have to cost a ton. Everyone will tell you to ride a bike, buy a hybrid, and install solar panels. But there are some smaller, lesser-known ways to make your routine Mother Nature approved.

Climate change: Tell me what I need to know.

Climate change is often referred to as reason number one we're on the Earth's sh*t list and the end of the world as we know it. It's a pretty straightforward concept: Humans burn fossil fuels (like coal and oil). That emits greenhouse gases that rise into the atmosphere and create a blanket around Earth. That blanket traps in heat . . . and leads to hotter temps. Aka global warming. Climate change causes everything from extreme weather to rising sea levels—both of which have gotten worse in the past few decades. Not good.

Thing to know
Climate change and global warming are not the same thing. While people often use them interchangeably, *global warming* refers to rising global temps. *Climate change* refers to all the effects of that—increased droughts, heat waves, extreme weather, coral reef deterioration, polar ice caps melting, etc. So global warming's like the sauna while climate change is like you sweating in it.

Don't some people say it doesn't exist?

Yes. Like many issues, it's political. Some people—mainly politicians and some special interest groups on the right—question whether climate change is man-made. Their argument is that the Earth has natural cycles of warming and cooling, and the human contribution factor is limited. But the large majority of scientists (around 97 percent of them) say that climate change is caused by humans.

How much worse has it gotten?

A lot. A 2018 UN report said the Earth's temp could rise by 2.7 degrees by 2040. That doesn't sound like a lot. But it could mean saying "bye" to coral reefs and "hi" to things like mass refugee crises. That's because severe weather patterns may cause people to flee their homes, creating global conflicts like migration crises.

In 2014, a Pentagon report said that climate change poses immediate risks to national security—the effects of climate change could seriously overwhelm the US's capability for disaster response. Meanwhile, Miami could be completely underwater by the end of this century if nothing's done to reverse the effects. And by 2050, a major storm event could flood nearly a quarter of NYC.

What's being done about all this?

World leaders are saying *bonjour* to a plan. In 2015, they got together in Paris and agreed on a plan to drastically reduce man-made emissions. Each country got its own targets to stop passing so much gas. Then, in 2017, President Trump announced that the US would withdraw from the deal. Because, in part, he campaigned on keeping coal and oil jobs. TBD on how all this will play out.

What can I do?

We all hear about reducing our carbon footprint. In practical terms, that means lowering the amount of carbon dioxide you release into the atmosphere from just living. Here are some things you can do in different areas of your life.

At home

For when your lightbulb goes out . . .

Replace it with an Energy Star–certified bulb. When you're shopping, make sure to look for that phrase on the label. A majority of US homes still use energy-inefficient lightbulbs. That's a socket to the face to Mother Nature. You might think, "One lightbulb will do nothing." Not so fast. If every house in the US replaced their bulbs with energy-efficient ones, the country would save enough energy to light two million homes for a whole year. It would also prevent greenhouse gas emissions equivalent to that of 550,000 vehicles. Shine bright, shine far.

For when you can't get comfortable . . .

Get with the program. Install a programmable thermostat (one where you can choose the exact temp). In the winter, for every degree you turn down the thermostat, you can save up to 3 percent off your heating bill. Plus, programmable thermostats don't use mercury like other thermostats, so they're more eco-friendly.

and rising

For when you're feeling a draft . . .

Seal the deal. Make sure your home is sealed. Energy savings from reducing drafts can be between 5 and 30 percent of a bill. Does that make you incensed? Make it literal. Use incense to test exactly where a draft is coming from. Where there's smoke, there's a draft. To fix it, get weather strips. We like the V-seal strips (easy) that you can order online. Cut them to the length of your window and apply along its outline.

take it back now, y'all

For when your ceiling fan looks lonely in the winter . . .

Flip it and reverse it. Instead of turning the heat way up, put your ceiling fan in reverse—so it's spinning clockwise. This pulls up cool air and pushes down warm air, so that you don't have to rely so much on energy-sucking heat.

For when you trip over your power cord . . .

Not feeling smart. Make sure the cord itself is. Get a smart power strip. Here's why: Devices that you plug into the wall—like your TV—actually keep using energy even when they are off. Instead of actually turning off, they go into "standby mode," which constantly uses energy and makes your bill higher. Smart power strips can do all the work for you by cutting all the power to things that are "off."

For when you're in the mood for sunny-side up . . .

Go solar. Solar panels are expensive. But it's worth noting that some states have solar-leasing programs, where you don't pay the cost of solar panels, equipment, and installation. Instead, you pay a monthly amount way lower than a regular electricity bill. Check to see if your state will help foot the bill.

For when you have an old iPhone 4 in your clutter drawer . . .

Recycle it. While recycling paper, cardboard, and plastic seems obvious, recycling electronics might not be as intuitive. Your tech is full of toxic stuff (like mercury and lead) that should never ever make it to a landfill. This material could leak into the environment and damage the ecosystem. Electronics recyclers collect, disassemble, repair, and recycle parts or metals from old electronics. Go to www.eiae.org to find out where you can get this done. And wipe your phone or laptop of all its data before recycling. The steps to do this are different for every device, so look yours up before recycling.

For when you're recycling the pizza box . . .

Don't. Paper or cardboard that's been stained by food can't be recycled. During the recycling process, that grease and oil can't be separated from the box's reusable fibers and will contaminate the actually recyclable paper it's processed with. Same goes for used paper plates and those paper towels you used to clean up a wine stain.

For when you have leftovers . . .

Compost up. This is a great way to reduce waste. Composting is breaking down organic matter to produce a nutrient-rich fertilizer. If you have a garden (we're impressed) it's a great way to improve your soil. Composting is easier outside. But you can do it inside too. Here are the steps to earn serious eco-friendly points.

1. Are you in or out?
Meaning inside or outside. If you're composting inside, you'll need to start with a compost bin, worms (yes), soaked paper strips, and soil. If you're doing it outside, you just need soil.

2. Collect the goods.
You'll need some browns (like eggshells, dead leaves, woodchips, and paper). And some greens (like veggie scraps, banana peels, and coffee grounds).

3. Layer up.
Switch from browns to greens to browns, etc.

4. Hydrate.
Add water to help break materials down.

5. Drop the remix.
Turn and mix everything once a week to circulate air through it. A hand rake or pitchfork will do the trick.

6. Repeat.
And be patient. Composting can take anywhere from a few weeks to a couple of years to finish.

At the store

For when you're going grocery shopping . . .

It's in the bag. The reusable bag. Get a reusable grocery bag and hang it on your door handle. That way, when you're leaving the house you won't forget it.

For when you're not sure how to read the label . . .

The words *organic* and *natural* get thrown around a lot. If you want to make sure you're buying the best products for the environment, go organic. There are few federal regulations regarding the word *natural.* But the USDA heavily regulates the use of *organic.* Pesticides, synthetic fertilizers, and GMOs (genetically modified organisms) need not RSVP to a 100 percent organic party. But not all organic products are created equal. Look for these distinctions on labels when you're shopping.

100 Percent Organic

The gold medal. This means the products are produced using only organic methods, and they contain only organic ingredients.

Organic

The silver. Products that contain at least 95 percent organic ingredients can use this one.

Made with Organic

The bronze. Products with 70 to 95 percent organic ingredients can wave this flag (label).

Organic food is almost always more expensive and better for the environment, but it's not always healthier. It's pesticide and antibiotic free but that doesn't always make it better nutritionally. Make sure to read the whole label and not just the organic badge.

For when you're buying seafood . . .

You'll hear a lot about wild caught vs. farm raised. Wild caught means it was caught, yup, in the wild by actual fishermen. Farm raised means it was raised commercially in a pond or tank. Farmed salmon is higher in fat, calories, and vitamin C. Wild-caught salmon is higher in minerals including potassium and iron. It also costs more. In general, wild caught is better for you, but it's a toss-up on which one is better for the environment. While wild caught is more natural and less metaphorically fishy, farm-raised fish prevent overfishing (removing fish from their home at a higher rate than they're reproducing). This can lead to underpopulation or extinction.

For when you're buying eggs . . .

Cage-free or **free-range**? A question almost as tricky as "Which came first, the chicken or the egg?" Both may sound like the chickens are roaming free in a field, à la *Charlotte's Web* or Maria in *The Sound of Music.* Lies. For cage-free, there's no space requirement for where the chicks can roam, meaning chicken producers can cram them into very tight spaces. Free-range is slightly better, since the chickens get outdoor access. The gold star goes to pasture-raised.

when did you get here?

For when you reach for the plastic . . .

That's the last straw. Really, really try to stop buying plastic water bottles and straws. Less than 6 percent of plastic actually gets recycled. And it's effing up our waterways and killing animals in the ocean. If you absolutely have to buy a plastic water bottle at some point, do not put it in the trash. Use it again or recycle it. Plastic bottles can take 450 years to decompose. And plastic bags clock in at around 1,000 years.

sip sip hooray

theSkimm: Climate change isn't just affecting the weather. The United Nations estimates that it's caused hundreds of thousands of deaths in recent years. The good news? It's in our power to turn the tide.

Skimm

MBA

"Do what you love and never work a day in your life" is BS. There's no way to succeed without working hard. But there are some tricks to help pave the way.

"SkimmMBA" is an overview of what you need to know to own your career. No advanced degree necessary. You'll get answers to questions about networking, resume building, interviewing, negotiating, and figuring out how to manage your time. Tick tock.

Things You Stalk

theSkimm on Networking

Networking is one of the most important business skills to have.

And you don't need to master any type of software to use it. It's essentially having strategic conversations, knowing how to follow up, and building a list of contacts that will have your back and give good advice. You have no choice but to network—it's not something you can opt out of.

You never know where a conversation may lead—a job tomorrow, a job in five years, or an introduction to a contact that will give you an opportunity. Spoiler: Most people like talking about themselves. You'll be surprised who's willing to tell you about his or her career in exchange for a cup of coffee.

Even if you don't nail it the first time—if someone doesn't respond, or says something like "Reach out to my office"—don't get discouraged. In some ways, networking is similar to dating. Here are some of the tactical steps you should always take to make sure you're building and keeping up with a network.

Profile Stalking: The Spreadsheet

Meet the stalker spreadsheet, no advanced Excel skills required. This is a way to make sure you're following up with your connections. Organize the spreadsheet with the connection's name in a cell of the left-hand vertical column. For each name, fill out these sections in header columns: contact info (email), title and company, the date you last connected, and notes. Go down this list and make sure to stay in touch with these people, and change the "Last connected" date accordingly. theSkimm recommends staying in touch with your most important connections at least once a quarter.

CONTACT	EMAIL	TITLE	LAST CONNECTED
Miranda Priestly	miranda.priestly @runway.com	Devil in Residence	Runway, Paris fashion week
Olivia Pope	olivia@opa.net	Executive White Hat	OPA, during a crisis
Bridget Jones	allbymyself @hotmail.com	Publicist @ Daniel Cleaver's bed	Ugly sweater party
Michael Scott	michael.scott @dundermifflin.com	"World's Best Boss"	Office christmas party

If you're worried about forgetting to keep up with these connections, there's automation for that. For your closest connections who you want to be seeing or speaking with once a quarter, tools like Zapier can send them variations of an automated email.

Swiping: The Blind Date

The most intimidating form of networking can be approaching or cold emailing a stranger. If you're emailing someone new, make sure you have a short email paragraph about yourself prepared in advance (just like you have your resume prepped for interviews).

That way your new connection can get a sense of who you are and why you want to get in touch.

If you're approaching a stranger at a networking event or a party, remember R&R. That does not stand for rest and relaxation.

Research

When you meet a VIP in your industry, chances are they won't remember you. Unless, that is, you mention something they've done recently or strike up a conversation about something specific. Look up their college or high school, if they're on any boards, where they are from, and recent press—all of these things will help build a connection. Saying "I really admire your work" sounds like you're talking to a B-list celeb whose movie you didn't actually watch.

Restraint

Don't hijack the conversation. You want people to remember you but not as "that person who didn't stop rambling." The best networkers are good at making other people feel special. Repeat: People like to talk about themselves. Look people in the eye. Say their name. Most important, listen . . . and mention something from your convo in your follow-up email. That brings us to . . .

Reconnecting: The Former Flame

A lot of people let good connections fade away because they think they have nothing new to say. That's probably not true. If you want a connection's perspective on a problem, that's something new. If you still don't know what you want to do with your career, but you figured out what you *don't* want to do, that's something new. What's the worst thing that can happen if you reach out again? They don't respond. Then you're back to where you were before. There's nothing to lose and a lot to gain in sending that email.

Set reminders to follow up with your most important connections at least once a quarter. You shouldn't save this for only when you're on the job search. Your contacts will be more likely to help you out if they get to know you and your career goals well through frequent check-ins. The most sincere and rewarding networking is done when you are genuinely curious and not looking for something beyond a person's time. The second time you follow up, simply respond to them through your original email conversation to make sure your connection has context for your meeting. After you've met twice, you can start sending fresh emails.

Flirting: The Follow-Up

After you meet with someone—whether it's a new or old connection—always make sure to follow up. Keep your follow-up email under 100 words and mention something you discussed together or something you admire about them. This is not a cover letter. It's a quick note that's basically saying "Hey, remember me?" Make sure to send your initial email within two days of your meeting—the sooner the better. Otherwise they won't remember your face (it's not your face's fault). Use "Best" as a sign-off. "Sincerely" somehow ironically sounds insincere.

New Number

Hi! It was so nice to meet you the other night. Sending you my resume.

New number...who is this?

The good ☒

Hi Katie,

It was great meeting you last night at the Young Marketers event. I loved hearing about the work you're doing at [insert company name], especially with the company's new product launch. Congrats! Have fun in LA this weekend. I'd love to grab coffee when you get back—let me know which times work best for you this month.

Best,
Alex

The bad

Hi Katie,

Great talking last night. Can you put in a good word with your boss? I'm super interested in [insert company name] and really think it would be a good fit. Here's my resume, let me know what she says!! Drinks soon??

Xoxo Alex

The first email is all about the receiver, while the second is all about the sender. It's also too casual. This person is not your friend (yet). Good connections take time to develop. Someone isn't going to give you a job after meeting you for five minutes.

Hanging Out with Each Other's Friends: Introductions

Networking is also about paying it forward. Once you start building a network, you become like a matchmaker. And you also become eligible for setups.

For when you're entry-level and get introduced to a new connection . . .

If you're getting connected to someone new via email, your connector may ask you to send a bio. If you're just starting out, your bio may actually require a bit more info. Since you have no solid experience in the real world, you'll need to illustrate why you're worthwhile to talk to.

Sample

I recently graduated from Colgate University with a double major in English and political science. While at school, I had a top-listened-to show on the campus radio station and interned at [insert company name] after my junior year. I would love to hear about your experience working in media, especially in podcast production.

For when you've had some experience and get introduced to a new connection . . .

The key word: brief. This is not your resume. Mention your full name, industry, current job title, and reason you want to be connected.

Sample

I am a senior account executive at [insert company name] with five years of PR experience. I'd love to hear about your work with hospitality clients, as I'm looking to break into that space.

And remember: If you're the one who asked for the introduction email, always respond to it first and move your connector to bcc. Sometimes people say, "Oh, I was waiting for the other person to respond." That's not how this works. When you ask to get set up, you make the first move.

For when you're asked to intro someone . . .

Make sure everyone involved has a heads-up before you send the intro email. Let's say Connection A (Beth, your former coworker in marketing) wants to meet Connection B (Maya, a business development exec) to talk about pivoting into business development. There are power dynamics at play here. You are asking a favor of Connection B and should email her first to make sure she's open to the introduction. Also, make sure to get a bio from Connection A before you make the ask.

Email Connection 101

Step 1

The email giving Connection B a heads-up should look something like this.

Hi, Maya,

I hope your summer's going well. I wanted to see if you'd be open to meeting my former colleague Beth Klein. She works as an integrated marketing associate, but is looking to learn more about the business development world. She's smart, scrappy, and was a pleasure to work with for two years.

Please let me know if you'd be willing to talk to her, and I'll make the connection. Hope to see you soon!

Best,
Kara

Step 2

If Connection B responds that she's willing to talk to Connection A, email them both. Make the subject line straightforward: Maya<>Beth Intro.

Hi, Maya,

I want to introduce you to my former colleague Beth. She works in marketing at [insert company name] and is looking to learn more about business development within the financial services space. She'd love to hear your perspective.

I'll let you two take it from here!

Best,
Kara

Step 3

Now it's on Beth (Connection A) to send the follow-up email and find a time that works for Maya (Connection B). Beth should be amenable to Maya's schedule and willing to meet her wherever is most convenient.

Step 4

Once you meet, make sure to keep your connector updated. In this example, Beth should email Kara thanking her for the setup and letting her know how the meeting went.

Playing the Field: Making New Connections

No matter what stage of your career you're in or how happy you are in your current role, you should constantly work on your network. No connection is too small. Who knows? Beth might offer Maya a job someday. One mistake people often make is not networking when they're happy at their job. Here are some ways to make sure you're always hustling.

For when you don't have time for more in-person coffee dates . . .

LinkedIn is your friend. And not your old friend who will be there no matter what. You have to work at this friendship. Make connections with people in the industry you're interested in, but don't mass connect. People will be able to tell if you're sending out a generic connection request that you sent to 200 others. Designate a day of the week to LinkedIn request everyone you met that week and start building an email list from there. You can send this list an update if you get a new job, start a business, etc.

For when you want to stand out . . .

Set up alerts on your connection. This might feel creepy, but it's not. If someone you look up to and want to work for does something big in the news, congratulate him or her. There's also an app called Accompany that compiles data and updates on big-time executives. Also look into apps like Shapr to meet new contacts.

Chandler Bing got a new job!

Say congrats!

For when you want to find someone's email . . .

Start with social. An email address is required to make an account on Facebook, Instagram, Twitter, and LinkedIn, so the person you're trying to contact may have their address there. If that's no dice, try using a tool like RocketReach.

theSkimm: Networking can be annoying. But it's necessary. So prepare to overcaffeinate and get it done.

Things You
Brag About
theSkimm on Your Resume

Think of your resume as a brag sheet and a pitch for why someone should hire you. No pressure.

Here's what any resume guide will tell you:

Less is more. Try to fit your resume onto one page.
Put your love on top. Use reverse chronological order and put your most recent and important accomplishments on top.
Spell it out. Use spell-check.
Format is key. Save it as a PDF. Otherwise, the formatting may become wonky when your potential employer opens it.

Thanks, Captain Obvious. You've heard people say all of those things. Now, here are our recommendations that go a bit beyond the basics.

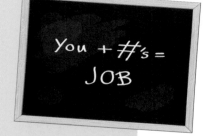

DO Play the Numbers Game

Remember when we told you to brag? Numbers will back it up. Not talking your salary. Talking about other numbers that showcase your value.

If you generated a lot of revenue for your last company, say how much. If you wrote for a site, say how much traffic your article received. Know your calculus: It says you plus numbers equals job.

DO Use Active Verbs

Produced, built, monitored. Go for unique ones like *maximized, consolidated,* and *administered* to stand out.

DO Say Mirror, Mirror

When it comes to cover letters, you can stand out by mirroring the voice of the company in your letter.

If you're applying for a job at a law firm, keep it formal. If you're applying for a job at a tech start-up with a laid-back culture, make your prose less stiff.

mirror mirror on the wall, who's the most employed of them all

DON'T

DON'T Objectify
Putting an "objective" at the top of your resume is becoming obsolete.

DON'T Put Your GPA on It
Unless it's your first or second job out of college and only if it's high. Many experts say that means 3.5 or higher. If you've been out of college for a while but received honors (cum laude, magna cum laude, summa cum laude), keep those on instead of your GPA.

DON'T State the Obvious
Avoid personal pronouns. Anyone reading it knows it's your resume. There is no "I" in *resume*.

Leave off "References available upon request." This is assumed, and it takes up valuable space.

Avoid phrases like *hard worker, ambitious, highly qualified, extensive experience, team player, people person, hit the ground running, think outside the box.* These should be a given and won't help convince someone to hire you.

DON'T Short Yourself
Eliminate short-term jobs (that is, those that lasted less than six months) from your resume, unless they directly relate to the position you are applying for.

If there are gaps in your resume, consider just putting the years you worked instead of the month and year. But if you were involved in something like an election or a community service–oriented role in between jobs, consider listing it instead of minding the gap. And including work in the hospitality or food service industry shows hustle and the ability to (literally) juggle many plates.

You need a resume. But your brag sheet should live on LinkedIn too. When it comes to that platform . . .

there's no "I" in resume

YOU MUST HAVE WORKED THIS LONG TO RIDE

RESUME

DO

DO Tell a Story

On LinkedIn, the "summary" portion of your profile is arguably the most important. And a lot of people don't even fill it out.

The summary lives right under your name, picture, and "headline" (current job and company).

It should be 100 to 200 words describing your experience and what you're currently seeking. Think of it like a less formal version of a cover letter.

The summary should hook a reader and tell a story. Use first-person—this should feel like the beginning of a convo.

Example: "I was a top salesperson at X company and brought in X revenue on a yearly basis. I am now looking to contribute my unique experience working with clients in X, X, and X industries to a growing and highly motivated team."

DO Keep It Consistent

The "Jobs" portion of your profile can be similar to your resume (active verbs, no personal pronouns). The summary is where you can state your objective and get a little more creative.

DO Engage

Posting articles (that you want your future employers to see) is a great way to show you're engaged and stay top of mind for people in your network.

https://www.linkedin.com

DON'T

DON'T Be Shy

Ask your current and former coworkers for recommendations. If you're just starting out, ask peers or professors. It takes two seconds and it's a thumbs-up for hiring managers and recruiters.

DON'T Photo Booth

Choose a professional picture. Professional wedding-goer does not count (no photo booth pics).

theSkimm: Your resume and LinkedIn profile are theSkimm of your career. Make sure they get right to the point.

Things That Make You Sweat

theSkimm on Interviewing

Interviewing is a production.

There's a lot that happens behind the scenes before showtime. And like performing, interviewing may make you want to throw up. Don't. Instead, follow these steps to make sure you are lights, camera, employed.

Rehearsal: The Prep

Practice makes perfect and nobody's perfect, but you still need to practice if you ever want a job. Preparing doesn't just mean selling yourself. It means stalking the company and its latest developments. People will tell you to look at the latest news about the company. But you should also read its blogs, check its social media accounts, and read its mission statement. And download or buy its products. When your interviewer asks about your familiarity with the company or its products, it's never a good look to admit you haven't used it. It's not a good idea to lie, either. Your potential employer can tell how long your nose is by looking up your purchase history, entering your email to see whether you're subscribed, etc.

Another big part of prepping? Coming up with your answers to some standard interview questions. Those might include . . .

of course
I've tried your
products before

Thing to know:
Always make sure to come prepared with questions. An interview is a dialogue. You need to find out if the company is right for you too. And if you don't have them, it looks like you're unengaged with the company and the position. Some smart questions include "How would you measure success in this role?" and "Why have people in this role not worked out in the past?"

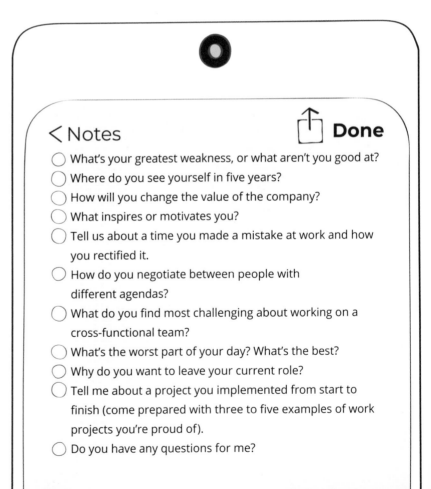

< Notes   ⬆ **Done**

- ◯ What's your greatest weakness, or what aren't you good at?
- ◯ Where do you see yourself in five years?
- ◯ How will you change the value of the company?
- ◯ What inspires or motivates you?
- ◯ Tell us about a time you made a mistake at work and how you rectified it.
- ◯ How do you negotiate between people with different agendas?
- ◯ What do you find most challenging about working on a cross-functional team?
- ◯ What's the worst part of your day? What's the best?
- ◯ Why do you want to leave your current role?
- ◯ Tell me about a project you implemented from start to finish (come prepared with three to five examples of work projects you're proud of).
- ◯ Do you have any questions for me?

There are some things you shouldn't say in response to these standard questions, which we'll get to below. Get *excitedddd*.

Show Day: Getting There

Because life is a journey, not a . . . you know the rest.

For when you're always late . . .

Late to a group dinner is one thing. Late to an interview is another. Everyone will tell you to be on time. But they might not tell you how exactly to make sure that happens. If your interview is at 11 and the office is a half hour away from you, make sure you leave at least 45 minutes before your interview. And schedule it as an event in your cal—with travel time—so you don't end up leaving too late. Aim to get there 10–15 minutes early. Because if you're on time for an interview, you're actually late.

For when the person at the front desk says "hi" . . .

Say "hi" back. One, because it's weird if you don't. And two, because feedback about you is likely being sent from everyone you interact with at the company. Seriously.

Performance: The Interview

It's go time.

For when you tend to ramble . . .

Meet the staying a-five list. This is your personal list of five bullet points to always keep in mind as your selling points. Here's an example of what they might look like at different career stages.

When you're starting out

Scrappy
Joined an on-campus group that met biweekly and increased membership by 10 percent within my first month as a member.

Creative
Put together an interactive presentation for [cough, insert class you took here], going above and beyond the assignment.

Organized
Never showed up late. Always completed assignments. Inbox zero is my friend.

Multitasker
Double majored and worked nights and weekends at a local restaurant. Can also highlight other extracurriculars here.

Brand affinity
I made 20 friends sign up for your service. I'm an early adopter to the product. Note: As an entry-level candidate, it's imperative to highlight why you'd be an excellent brand advocate and understand the company's products.

When you've been working for years

Visionary
Created a new product that grew company's revenue by 10 percent.

Manager
Grew a team of direct reports from two to four in less than three months. Promoted a direct report after advocating internally for her.

Communicator
Conducted weekly one-on-ones with team members and with my boss. Skilled at managing up.

Organized
Project-managed and streamlined processes for my team to cut down time dedicated to a project by 20 percent.

Brand affinity
I'm an early user of your company's product. I worked for a similar product [cough, insert your strategy here, cough].

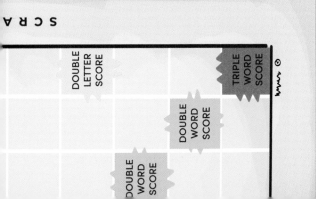

For when you don't know how to answer the "greatest weakness" question . . .

Yer not a wizard. You can't use a wand to turn a weakness into a strength. If you try to, your interviewer might call BS. It's more genuine to use something you're actually working on, rather than a humblebrag like "working too hard" or "being a perfectionist" that any employer will likely see through. Be honest, but make sure to present your weaknesses strategically. Instead of saying you're a "bad communicator" or "resistant to criticism," think about what those weaknesses really mean. They may indicate that you want to work on delegating and separating emotion from work. Presenting your weaknesses in a different light can show how deeply you care about your job, have a lot on your plate, and are working toward improving as a manager.

WEAKNESSES

STRENGTHS

Reviews: The Follow-Up

Send a thank you email on the same day. Just do it. Make sure to mention something specific you discussed in the interview. If you really, really want the job, it doesn't hurt to also send a handwritten thank-you note. But the email is crucial, since it helps make your case more immediately.

theSkimm: "Be yourself" is good interview advice with one caveat: Be the version of yourself you'd want to hire.

Things That Need
Talking Out

theSkimm on Negotiating

Negotiating is like verbal dancing.

And you don't want to end up on your back foot (or looking like your uncle doing the "YMCA"). But if you anticipate your negotiating partner's needs and don't fall over, you may end up with a higher paycheck. Here we'll cover salary negotiations both for jobs you're interviewing for and when you've worked at a company for years.

How should I negotiate when I'm job searching? 🔍

Wait until an offer's on the table before you negotiate. And once you get the offer, don't negotiate on the spot. Ask for one or two days to think through the pros/cons of the job and come up with a strategy to negotiate. More on that strategy later. You should be considering a LOT of things when it comes to deciding whether to take a job. These include salary, title, stock options, moving expenses, 401(k) plans, health benefits, vacation days, and professional development ops.

For when your potential employer asks about your current salary . . .

Depending on where you live, this may be illegal. That's because of the gender wage gap. The thinking is that forcing candidates to report their salaries unfairly penalizes women, who statistically make less cash money than men. California, Delaware, Massachusetts, and Oregon say nope to the salary question. So do NYC, Philly, Pittsburgh, and New Orleans. If it *is* legal where you live, it's a good idea to try to find out the budget for the position first. You can phrase this as "I'd love to first hear about the budget for this role, so I can make sure it's in line with my salary expectations." Once you get a sense of that, mention *your* salary expectations, aka what it would take for you to accept the job.

Reply hazy, your Q is illegal

Talk is cheap

For when you get a verbal promise . . .

Talk can be cheap. Make sure you get everything in writing—including the job offer and any compensation promises—before updating your LinkedIn profile or counting on that extra cash. For instance, if a company promises an annual bonus, but it's not part of your offer letter . . . don't get too excited for that icing on your end-of-year cake.

How should I negotiate in general?

There are a couple of different things to keep in mind.

For when you're trying to organize your thoughts . . .

Know what's important to you. Is it cash? **Equity?** Benefits and perks? You rarely get the ideal in all three, so whether you are negotiating your salary at a current job or at a new one, make it clear to the hiring manager what you care most about. That will make his or her job easier, and the outcome for you even better.

For when you just need to get it off your chest . . .

Much like love, one-liners, and catching a train, timing is everything. Make sure you choose your moment wisely. If you're asking for a raise at your current company, do not ask right after your boss did something nice for you, right after your boss gave you critical feedback, or when the business appears to be under unusual stress (like during the launch of a new product, closing a sales cycle, or raising money). But if you believe you deserve a raise and you're happy at your current company, don't look for a competing offer just to bring a negotiating chip to the table. It creates a contentious environment for the conversation right off the bat.

For when you're prepping for the conversation . . .

80 percent of the work you do should happen before you walk
into the room. Here's a look at points you should hit on in your prep
and pitch. Remember "MINE"—because that cash money will soon
be just that.

M **Market rates**

Know yours. There is a lot of third-party data you can get from sites like PayScale,
Glassdoor, and Salary.com. But be careful. For instance, in the tech industry, these sites
don't take company stage into account and can lead to market confusion. Make sure you
are getting your information about positions at similar companies in similar stages. To do
this, check things like how much funding and how many employees a company has.

I **Illustrate**

Brag about your accomplishments. Break out that brag sheet and treat this like an
interview. Then create a 30, 60, and 90-day plan of how you will tackle certain
company aims, given new job responsibilities and a raise. Present those plans during
your meeting.

N **Negotiate**

Be specific. The first number you give is the most important, and it should be on
the upper end of your range. Never provide your range, as that's an invitation to pay
you at the lower end.

E **Earn**

Get that cash money. But also be willing to walk away. If you have
another offer on the table, only mention it if you're willing to take
the competing offer.

What should I avoid doing?

There are a lot of things you should do when negotiating. But there are also a lot of things you should avoid.

For when you're applying for an entry-level position . . .

This might not be the right time to ask for more money—unless you have data that indicates that the offer is off-market. To lean in, you have to first have something to lean on. Once you get that first job, then you should negotiate for your next one, or for your next promotion.

For when you're worried the salary won't cover your living expenses . . .

Avoid TMI. Do not get into your specific needs with your potential employer. That is, don't say, "My rent is going up so I need a higher salary" or "I have student loans to pay off so you should pay me more." They should want to pay you more based on the worth you'll bring to the company, not only based on your personal needs. Those needs can help inform what you ask for in negotiations, but it's important to negotiate with your employer in mind as well.

For when this doesn't change the fact that your salary doesn't cover your living expenses . . .

Pursuing your passion vs. paying your bills is a real debate, especially when you're starting out. You may need to pick up a side hustle to cover gaps in that starting salary. Here are some ideas to look into.

Dog walking

Apps like Wag are an easy way to get some extra cash and extra time with dogs.

Babysitting

Check out sites like Sittercity and Care.com, or go old school and put up a flyer in your building. The neighbors will thank (and pay) you.

Tutoring

Through places like Kaplan and TutorMe, you can set up a side hustle teaching kids to read, etc.

Sell sh*t

Sell household items on sites like eBay. Sell clothes on places like Poshmark.

Get cash back

Shop through places like Ebates to get cash back on things you buy.

Focus groups

Get paid for your opinion. Companies like Probe Market Research, Engage, and 20|20 Panel offer money in exchange for your two cents on products. And they pay more than two cents. This will usually get you $50 to $400 depending on the time commitment and product.

For when you're tempted to compare yourself while negotiating . . .

Don't do it. It's not a good look to say "So and so moved up; when is my turn?" or "I know so and so makes more than me." This ends up doing the exact opposite of your intention. It makes you look small and gossipy, and it does not inspire goodwill.

we need to talk

theSkimm: A job offer is the start of a conversation. Make sure you're prepared to get what you want out of it.

Things That Help You

Own It

theSkimm on Career Pep Talks

Even the people at the top—your boss's boss's boss and the VIPs in your news feed—don't know what they're doing a lot of the time.

Or think they don't. Imposter syndrome is real. But the syndrome doesn't need to have noticeable symptoms.

While being vulnerable and asking questions makes sense in certain situations, there are ways to channel confidence even when you're not feeling it. Here are some words and phrases to avoid, to make sure you're presenting the sitting-up-straight version of yourself.

The P-word: Protective Words

Just. Just don't use it. It diminishes the words that follow. Instead of "Just following up," write "I'm following up."

I think or *IMO.* These are words you might use to try to protect yourself before you wreck yourself, but they actually end up undermining your power.

Yeah, but comes across as combative and negative.

The S-word: Superlatives

The most amazing, the greatest, and even *the best* sound a *liiittle* like you're on uppers. They're so hyperbolic that they don't feel genuine.

Use more precise phrasing. Instead of "This would be the greatest deal" say "This deal would contribute to our mission and bring in enough dollars to meet our Q3 revenue goal."

The D-word: Dramatic Words

Totally, very, absolutely. These types of words can diminish your credibility and make you sound like Cher Horowitz.

The F-word: Filler Words

Like, whatever, etcetera, so on, and *so forth.* Pause for a moment to collect your thoughts. Then, like, don't fill the space with fillers.

The A-words: Ability and Apology Words

I'll try. Trying suggests you're unsure of your ability to complete the task.

Sorry. Use it sparingly for situations directly caused by you. Don't apologize for instances out of your control or for someone else's actions. Also, never criticize or apologize for your own work while making a presentation (for example, "Sorry if you can't read this slide well.") It delegitimizes your work before you get going.

The other S-word: Superior Words

Actually and *obviously* suggest that people don't understand the issue or circumstances. They're condescending.

Like I said and *as I've believed all along* make you sound defensive.

That's not my job makes you sound kind of lazy. Rather than say it explicitly, reroute the task to someone whose job it is.

just, like, actually
don't use them,
etcetera

For when you want to pick up new business skills . . .

Go for it. The easiest way to start is by shadowing people in the department you want to learn more about. If your boss gives you the green light, reach out to someone in that department and see if you can be a fly on the wall. If you want to learn a really specific skill—coding, Excel, or graphic design, for instance—consider taking a course. Places like General Assembly, Coursera, and Codeacademy offer a wide range of options.

For when you need a pep talk . . .

Look to those you admire for a pick-me-up. Here are some favorite quotes from women who've made their mark, as told to theSkimm.

It's really important to give people autonomy... to let people really be in control of the work that they do.

— Ariel Kaye, founder and CEO of Parachute

My life isn't less busy or less full of things. What has changed is my prioritization.

— Arianna Huffington, founder and CEO of Thrive Global

Always go above and beyond the call of duty – Nobody's ever penalized for doing more than what's expected of their job. Somebody always notices.

— Gayle King, co-anchor, CBS This Morning & editor at large at O, The Oprah Magazine

My biggest mistake has been saying "yes" too much.

— Lauren Bush Lauren, co-founder and CEO of FEED Projects

I tell her not to give so much power to her doubts. I tell her not to give so much credence to the negative thoughts. The more you let yourself go down negative spirals, the more you let yourself be motivated by fear.

— Leandra Medine, founder of Man Repeller, on what she'd tell her 21-year-old self.

If you fail, so what? Its better than never doing it at all. If you never do something, then you've already failed. ... What's better than zero? Even 1% is.

— Whitney Wolfe Herd, founder and CEO of Bumble

Everyone has a voice if they choose to use it.

— Margaret Brennan, moderator of CBS's *Face the Nation*

The worst advice I've ever gotten is to wait my turn, to start small. I think women are told that a lot. And I'm glad I didn't listen.

— Reshma Saujani, founder and CEO of Girls Who Code

You can't be afraid to walk away. When you know your worth, and you know what you have to offer, it may take you longer to get where you're going but if you have something offer you will get there.

— Taraji P. Henson, award-winning actress and activist

BE CAREFUL ABOUT LISTENING TO TOO MANY PEOPLE. BE CURIOUS AND OPEN AND SEEK LEARNING FROM OTHERS, BUT ULTIMATELY YOU OWN YOUR DECISIONS.

—TY HANEY, FOUNDER AND CEO OF OUTDOOR VOICES

THERE'S NEVER A _GOOD_ TIME. I OFTEN
MENTOR YOUNG WOMEN WHO ARE LIKE
"I WANNA HAVE A BABY, GET MARRIED, OR
START A COMPANY, BUT I CAN'T DO THAT
UNTIL XYZ."

WHAT IF NONE OF THIS HAPPENS?...
YOU'VE GOT TO DRIVE FORWARD.

— JENNY FLEISS,
CO-FOUNDER OF RENT THE RUNWAY
CEO OF JETBLACK

It's healthy to disagree.
challenge each other. Push back.
But then commit to a
decision & move forward together.

— Shan-Lyn Ma,
founder & CEO of Zola

I used to call my
dad crying. And he
would always say,
"What makes metal
steel? Extreme heat,
baby." And he was right.

—Melissa Ben-Ishay,
president and chief
product officer at
Baked by Melissa

Those moments that you push
yourself to do something you
may not be great at... have
so many hidden gifts in them
that to not do them would be
such a shame.

— Sara Blakely, founder and
CEO of Spanx

If it doesn't feel like there's
another seat at the table,
dammit, drag another seat out.

—Rebecca Minkoff, co-founder
and creative director of Rebecca
Minkoff LLC

Say what you want. Say it out loud, and say it to your supervisor and HR. People are busy, or misguided by your gender, or simply can't guess what you want. The first step to the next step is to say what you want.

— Fiona Carter, chief brand officer at AT&T

Stop looking for "why not" and start looking for "why yes." There is always a solution; you just have to find it!

— Shelley Zalis, CEO of The Female Quotient

Put me out of my comfort zone. Put me in a place where I stand out most. Back me into a corner... that's when I do my best work.

— Christina Tosi, founder and CEO of Milk Bar

You have to want to follow someone who tells you no. You don't want the yes' person who doesn't wanna hurt anyone's feelings. You want the person who tells you no.

— Hoda Kotb, Emmy award-winning co-anchor of the Today Show and NYT bestselling author

IT'S INCREDIBLY EMPOWERING, THOUGH QUITE DIFFICULT, TO JUST SAY THE WORD "NO."

— JOANNA COLES, FORMER CHIEF CONTENT OFFICER AT HEARST MAGAZINES

A bad day for your ego is a great day for your soul.

—Jillian Michaels, author and fitness expert

You know your value. You know your worth. If you're outside the door and you're knocking...go in with confidence and knowing that you have just as much right to be there as they do. If they're not answering—build your own house.

—Arlan Hamilton, founder and managing partner of Backstage Capital

I have always been mission-obsessed, not product-obsessed. That's the path to making sure you're solving what you set out to do.

—Payal Kadakia, founder and executive chairman of ClassPass

If you want a bigger job, make your own job bigger.
—Kristin Lemkau, chief marketing officer at JPMorgan Chase

Of course you can [do it]. You're just going to be tired for years.

—Sallie Krawcheck, cofounder and CEO of Ellevest on advice from her mom.

Be able to stand on your own two feet...
have confidence in your own abilities, and
everything else will be the icing.
— Gregg Renfrew, founder
and CEO of Beautycounter

I learned negotiation has
nothing to do with price.
It has everything to
do with ego and timing.
— Barbara Corcoran, Shark
Tank "Shark" and co-founder
of Forefront Venture Partners

Don't let perfect stop you.
Don't let it get in the way of good.
— Linnea Roberts,
founder + CEO of
Gingerbread Capital

You're going to get criticism and hate
no matter what, especially when you're
putting yourself out there... not everyone's
going to love (you), which is fine."
— Arielle Charnas, founder of
Something Navy

My currency is learning.
It's not title.
It's not money.
I give ZERO shits about those things.
— Kat Cole,
President and COO of FOCUS Brands.

I have this rule of thumb in life. If you hear about something three times, then you have to go and either do it, eat it, or read it.

→Melanie Whelan, CEO of SoulCycle

I don't really feel that I've truly been prepared 100% for anything I've done. And I think that's a good thing.

—Mindy Grossman, president and CEO of WW

Being an optimist, you don't hear a lot of the bad. You try to hear the good, get the good, and make sure you're living up to that good.

—Martha Stewart, founder of Martha Stewart and host of "Martha & Snoop's Potluck Dinner Party"

I'm a believer in building networks of _smart people_, rather than _looking for a_ single mentor.

—Christie Hefner, former CEO and chairman of Playboy Enterprises

I'm a big believer in taking the job no one else wants.... I believe a lot in intuition and seeing opportunities in jobs that other people don't like.

—Beth Comstock, former vice chair of GE and author

If you ask 90-year-olds what they regret in life, they regret the things they didn't do, not the things they did.
— Alexa von Tobel, founder and managing partner of Inspired Capital

You're going to have a lot of chances to define who you wanna be professionally. It's not a straight line. And that's exciting. Once you realize that, the choice you make now... is not the end of the story.
— Susan Lyne, founder and President of BBG Ventures.

You don't leave the site of a sale until you've heard 'no' three times... That [advice] has opened up many opportunities for me.
— Sylvia Acevedo, CEO of Girl Scouts

theSkimm: You need to advocate for yourself. No one else is going to do it for you. Breathe, look in the mirror, and say, "Let's do this."

Things That Are
Ticking

theSkimm on Time Management

Time is the one that got away . . . or the one you have to learn to tame.

theSkimm is all about making your time well spent. Most people and self-help books will tell you to carpe diem and make the most of your hours. We will tell you actual ways to squeeze in all the things you have to do.

How do I get it all done?

Here are some tricks to feel more on top of those 17-ish hours you're awake.

For when your to-do list looks like a sad handwritten book . . .

Meet the **1-3-5 list.** It's a way to make your to-do list less scary by checking off one big thing, three medium-sized things, and five small tasks on any given day. Because doing something easy first gives you the confidence to keep going.

For when your coworker's ringtone keeps going off . . .

Put your own ring on it. As in, timed blocks of work (delineated by an alarm) can help avoid distractions. The **Pomodoro technique**—named because the guy who invented it had a timer in the shape of a tomato—might be your secret sauce. Here's how it works: Work without distractions for a timed 25-minute block. Take a five-minute break. Repeat. After four 25-minute working sessions, take a half-hour break to stay creative and move around. Or to watch a YouTube video featuring puppies. Warning: Maybe don't do this in front of your boss.

For when you get in the zone . . .

You might need more than 25 minutes to focus in. **90-minute blocks** have also been proven to help with focus and concentration. Think of this like responsible binge watching—one and a half episodes at a time.

For when you spend half your day responding to emails . . .

Play hard to get. Unless the email requires an immediate response, designate a few 30-minute blocks a day for catching up on email. That way, you can get actual work done without a "You've got mail" distraction.

For when your phone notifications are giving you heart palpitations . . .

Turn. Them. Off. Turning off notifications or putting your phone on Do Not Disturb is surprisingly satisfying. Warning: Do not panic when you finally look at your phone. It won't bite. Hard.

For when you need a break . . .

Treat yourself. That means: Take a walk, read an article, grab lunch.

Get sh*t done

For when it feels like most of your day is taken up by meetings or networking . . .

Learn a very important two-letter word: No. It's important to know when to put yourself first. Go to your manager and tell him or her you need a block of time to get something done. Tell a contact that this month is busy and ask to get something on the calendar next month instead. People will appreciate your honesty, and you'll appreciate the extra time.

feed me

theSkimm: Time management makes productivity makes career success makes money. It's physics 101. While our careers are more than just our paychecks, the paycheck doesn't hurt. And with great power comes great financial responsibility. It's time to talk about the piggy bank in the room.

Does it ever feel like some of your friends have taken secret classes or training on how to manage money and save? Surprise: They're probably struggling in similar ways. If they aren't, good for them. Insert fake smile.

"Skimm Money" will give you the good cents (see what we did there?) to make smart decisions about your bank account. You'll learn about putting together a budget, paying off student loans, doing your taxes, buying a house, and more. This sounds like it will hurt, but everything's going to be OK.

Things That
Save Money

theSkimm on Budgeting and Savings

If looking at your bank account feels like getting back a test you know you failed . . . you're not alone.

Budgeting is the key to feeling financially secure, but no one really teaches you how to do it in school. You may be wondering, "How did no one ever tell me the right way to do this?" No time like right now.

We've broken this up into a few categories: general budgeting and savings, paying off loans, and saving up for the big stuff. That includes retirement.

How do I get started?

Here are five main steps to making a budget. Remember the mnemonic **I** **G**o **F**ar **T**o **M**ake **M**oney.

Income: Figure out your **net income**. To do this, take your salary and subtract deductions. That includes things like income tax, Social Security, health insurance premiums, and your 401(k). If you have a full-time job, your employer will do this subtraction for you. You'll see that amount as your **adjusted gross income,** or how much you take home after deductions. Your **gross income** is how much your boss told you you'd make.

Goals: Set goals. Do you want to pay off your student loans? Save up for a home? Start with one big goal and write down the magic number that corresponds with it.

Fixed expenses: Calculate your fixed, necessary monthly expenses. These are your "need it" expenses that stay fixed month-to-month. That includes rent, utilities, and transportation.

Tracking: For a month, break down everything you spend that's not a fixed expense. These are your "want it" expenses. That includes clothes and travel. Be specific so you know exactly where you're spending, and where you can cut down. Don't just say "$350 on food and dining." Instead, get all up in your receipts: coffee: $40; groceries: $80; dinners out: $110; lunches: $120.

Math Minute: After a month of stalking your receipts, subtract your expenses (both "need it" and "want it" expenses) from your monthly salary. Is that number negative or positive? Are you spending more than you're making, or do you have some cash money left over?

If it's positive . . . start saving. Calculate how long it will take you to get to your savings goal in step 2 if you save $50 a month vs. $100 a month vs. $200 a month vs. . . . you get the picture. Experts recommend saving between 10 and 20 percent of your take-home pay. That might seem daunting, especially when you have student loans to pay off. Start with 5 percent. Even 1 percent. Just start somewhere.

*lettuce pray...
for your
wallet*

If it's negative . . . take a red pen to your "want it" expenses. If you're spending too much on food, people will tell you to stop buying things that go bad before you eat them (looking at you, head of lettuce) and start saying no to big group dinners. We think you should get more granular than that. Take the top two biggest monthly food expenses from your list (for example, lunches and dinners out) and try to cut those expenses by 10 percent. If you can do that, graduate to 20 percent the next month. Keep going until you've chopped your two biggest expenses in your most spend-happy category in half.

I can't decide where to cut down . . .

No one said budgeting was easy. Here are some factors to consider.

For the person who likes clear rules . . .

Try the **50/30/20 rule**. Here's how it works: Half your paycheck goes to things you need (the "need it" expenses, like rent). If you live in a major city this might be tricky to keep at just half. Another 30 percent goes to things you want (the "want it" expenses, like wine and plane tickets). And 20 percent goes to paying off debt or to savings and investing.

How much cash money should be in my savings account?

People say you should have enough money to cover three to six months' worth of essentials (your "need it" expenses, like rent) saved up. This gives you some cushion in case you lose your job or need to take on extra expenses. People also say that by 30, you should aim to have the equivalent of your annual salary saved up. Thank you for that advice. But it seems pretty unrealistic. Start with saving three months' worth of essentials and see how that goes.

For when you're not meeting your savings goal . . .

First things first. As in, transfer your monthly goal amount to your savings account at the beginning of the month. To take it a step further, set it and forget it: Set up automatic, recurring savings transfers with your bank. Every month, your money should be making moves (from your checking to your savings).

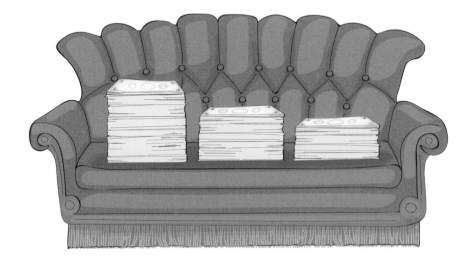

What if I have student loans?

Ah, the debt-ridden elephant in the room. If you have student loans to repay, you are very much not alone. There is over $1.5 trillion in student loan debt in the US. And the average graduating senior has over $35,000 in debt. But since you're a human who needs food and shelter, you can't put all your money toward that debt.

congrats now pay us back

So then how do I pay off my loans, exactly?

As soon as you can. It may take years but don't get discouraged. Most people recommend making it a number one money priority after graduation. Here are some methods to try.

For the person who likes to check off small items from their to-do list first . . .

Let it snow. As in, try the **snowball method.** Pay your smallest debts first, regardless of interest rate. Start by listing out all your debts, smallest to largest. Pay the minimum balance on each one, except the smallest. For that one, dedicate as much cash to it as possible each month until it's repaid. Then put that payment amount toward the second smallest debt, and so on. The idea? You'll gain momentum by watching your debts disappear. *Aaand* it snowballs from there.

For the person who likes to jump in headfirst . . .

Sound the avalanche whistle. The **avalanche method** focuses on paying down debts with the highest interest rates first. It minimizes the amount of interest you're paying overall, which can save you thousands over time, depending on how much debt you have.

Thing to know
APY. Stands for annual percentage yield, or the yearly rate of return of the money in your savings account. Accounts with better interest rates have a higher APY.

For the person who doesn't like when their meat touches their potatoes . . .

Keep it separate. Make a separate savings account where you set aside part of your paycheck just for student loan payments. It'll make it easier not to touch that money for other things.

What type of savings account should I get?

It depends. Here are some of the different ones you can open with your bank.

Standard: The tried-and-true. This is the type of savings account most Americans have. Some have zero or low minimums.

Do this if . . . you're starting out and don't have a lot of money to put into the account. Interest rates are low on standard accounts.

CD: Not that kind. This is a certificate of deposit. Banks often let you open a special kind of account with better rates than you would get in a regular savings account. But you have to keep your hands off that money for a certain amount of time (usually a few months up to a few years).

Do this if . . . you won't need to access that money for the period, and you want a "can't touch this" way for your cash to earn interest.

High-yield savings account: An account where you put more in and get more back. The interest rates are often higher, but you usually need to invest a certain amount to get one.

Do this if . . . you have more money to invest and want the flexibility of withdrawing it at any time.

PS: You can negotiate for a better interest rate on your account by finding competing offers from other banks. Bring them up to your bank for a chance at getting a better rate.

This is a lot. Will I ever be able to retire?

Saving for retirement is kinda like eating right. It's annoying and feels unrealistic in the short term, but it has long-term benefits. That may sound like BS but it's true.

Here are some of the retirement savings terms and concepts you'll come across and the benefits of each.

401(k): An employer-sponsored retirement savings plan. It lets you save and invest a piece of your paycheck before taxes are taken out. You won't be taxed on it until you start withdrawing the money (hint: That's why you shouldn't withdraw until you retire). Some companies will match how much you contribute to your 401(k) up to a certain amount. This is free money. If it still sounds scary to set a piece of your paycheck away, know that you'll have options for how to invest it. One common option is to park it in a target-date fund that tweaks your investments over the years based on what year you plan to retire. So as you get older, your 401(k) spread will become less risky.

Do this if . . . your company offers it. Especially if they offer to match your contributions. Every company's plan is different, so read the fine print. One example: A company might match 100 percent of your contributions up to 5 percent. Translation: For every dollar you decide to put toward your 401(k), your company will put a dollar into it too, up to 5 percent of your salary before tax deductions.

IRA: Individual retirement account. There's a max amount you can contribute to an IRA each year—it's $6,000 for 2019, but typically goes up a little every few years. Like with a 401(k), you decide how you want to invest it. If you do a traditional IRA, you hit snooze on paying taxes on the money until you take it out. If you do a **Roth IRA,** you'll pay the taxes up front. Some experts say it's better to do a Roth IRA, since you don't have to pay taxes when you withdraw all that money that's been gathering interest for years. It's also advised to invest your money into your IRA or Roth IRA at the beginning of the year, so it has the chance to gain interest over the year.

Do this if . . . your company doesn't offer a 401(k), or if you're maxing out your 401(k) and want to put aside even more money for retirement. Or if you just want to pay less taxes now while saving up for the future.

theSkimm: Budgeting is a b-word. But it will result in the savings you need in the long run—which means extra money in the bank and cash to invest.

5.26   421.79   219.91   173.72   236.

6" Invest in "me-time" Invest in

94   513.67   617.66   214.85   83.87

e-time" Invest in your future. No pre

74.98   212.55   1023.92   146.67   6.

vest in "self-care" Invest in "me-

.89   77.11   511.94   87.22   101.45

me" Invest in your future. No pressu

11.87   76.54   1003.61   101.73   39.

ure. No pressure. Invest in "self-

303.56   1016.91   456.97   218.76

in "me-time" Invest in your future

123.87   105.97   1122.60   208.87

essure. Invest in "self-care" Inve

45   278.98   430.91   78.45   135.6

Things That
Make You Money

theSkimm on Investing

You've heard "Invest in your future," "Invest in your happiness," and "Invest in me-time." Great. Thanks for that.

We are told to invest in many things, but investing actual money, and how to get it done the smart way, leaves a question mark in a lot of people's minds. Studies have shown that most millennial women feel like they don't have enough money to start investing, and say they want to be more educated on investing before they start doing it. So here we are.

OK, then. How do I get started?

Easy as 1, 2, 3 . . .

Stay account(able).

Open a **brokerage account:** You can open one online with places like Charles Schwab, Vanguard, or ETrade. To get it going, you'll need your Social Security number and your driver's license. In most states, you also have to be 18. Once you've set up an account, you'll need to transfer money into it to start investing. Use the 50/20/30 method from before as a guide. Think of this like the garden where you're going to plant your investments. And watch your money grow. Experts say you should check it no more than once a quarter. You don't want to make knee-jerk decisions based on a good or bad quarter.

Phone a friend.

If you want help, you can have a real live human financial advisor step in. You can find this person through the site you used for your brokerage account. Tell your advisor what your goals are with your portfolio—what do you want to use this money for? Make sure to ask them questions like "How much risk am I exposed to?" and "What's my all-in fee?"—if your advisor puts your money in funds managed by third parties, they may charge fees that aren't mentioned up front.

Plant the seeds.

Start choosing the types of investments you want to grow. Green thumb in more ways than one.

What are my options?

There are lots of different crops (had to, we'll stop now) you can choose from. Here are some of the most popular and why they might be right for you.

Mutual funds: Instead of trying to pick your own stocks, you buy a mutual fund made up of many stocks. Mutual funds consist of many stocks, bonds, or both. They're professionally managed by investment firms. Sometimes they're focused on a specific category of company; other times the firm tries to pick the companies they believe will perform the best. You'll likely see mutual funds as investment options in your 401(k) at your job. But you can also buy into mutual funds on your own. These are options you'll be able to pick in your new brokerage account.

Try this if . . . you want to get started but also want a financial whisperer to help. Mutual funds are controlled by a team of portfolio managers who do this for a living. You won't have voting rights to make decisions in the fund, but that might be a good thing if you're still getting your financial feet wet. They're also pretty low cost. The minimum amount you have to invest may vary by fund, and can be as low as $100.

ETFs . . . similar to mutual funds, ETFs (exchange-traded funds) are made up of a variety of things (think: stocks and bonds). Most ETFs are set up to focus on a specific category of companies, such as the 500 largest US stocks (aka the S&P 500 index, which we'll get into later). And unlike mutual funds, ETFs are traded daily on stock exchanges, and their prices fluctuate throughout the day. They typically have much lower costs than other investments, because they don't require a professional to be as hands-on. They also typically have no or low minimum-investment amounts, so you can get started ASAP in your brokerage account.

Try this if . . . you don't want to pay (too much) to play. This is the lowest cost option and the most flexible. Because they're traded like stocks, you can pull out of or trade ETFs at any time during the day.

the feeling's mutual

Bonds: One way for a company or the government to raise money. Here's how it works: You give a large company or the gov money, and they are indebted to pay you back, at fixed interest rates (aka stable payments and no surprises). It's basically a "You scratch my back, I scratch yours" situation, except your scratch turns into a massage if the investment is good. The level of risk depends on the issuer, because if you're issued a bond from a company that ends up failing, you'll get nada. Bonds are less risky than stocks since they're typically issued from large corporations and the gov, and have a defined payment schedule. Your 401(k) may be partially invested in bonds. Note: If you're getting a corporate bond, you'll still have to pay taxes on the interest payments you receive. If it's a government bond, the interest is tax-exempt. Look at you go.

Try this if . . . you want to add some diversity to your portfolio. Bonds are generally a steady bet, and their return doesn't fluctuate with the market like stocks do. But their return also isn't known for being super high. If you're young (or like to live dangerously) it's best to put more of your cash money into . . .

Stocks: When you own a small piece of a public company. It's a way to take, yup, stock in the co. and gives you the opportunity to reap its benefits. Owning stock means you benefit when the company's earnings are up. But you also lose out when the company's in the red. If you have a 401(k), you're probably already invested in stocks. Aka you don't need to buy individual stocks to get in on this kind of investing.

Try this if . . . you've done your research. Buying individual stocks on your own is risky, because you need a LOT of them to get the type of diversification you'll find in a mutual fund or ETF. But if you buy individually, you do pay less in fees than you would for a mutual fund or ETF, since there's no financial advisor helping you along the way.

3.72	173.72	173.7		173.72	173.72	173.72	173.72	173.7
	234.85	235.56	381.45	358.87	685.14	237.05	239.81	439.58
483.23	214.79	729.29	325.98	685.73	146.57	352.88	594.38	475.38
938.65	491.47	352.71	643.80	587.14	754.78	235.79	436.86	184.72
347.94	664.67	421.79	235.98	685.84	346.78	367.28	436.08	890.54
594.32	235.08	652.79	230.82	859.47	236.64	438.57	658.38	347.07
2.72	173.72	173.7	173.72	173.72	173.72	173.72	173.72	173.7

Does a good stock market mean a good economy and vice versa?

Short answer: not necessarily. The day-to-day fluctuations of the stock market do not have much bearing on the economy as a whole. But over time, stock market trends will reflect the state of the economy. Think of it like a relationship: Fights here and there don't mean you're headed for a breakup. But if you're fighting every day and sleeping in different rooms, it's a bad sign. By the time the economy is in **recession,** the stock market will have been in a long decline.

When should I invest?

When the market's on an upswing. It's generally a good idea to get into new investments during a **bull market**—aka when prices are steadily increasing and you have a chance to ride that wave. On the opposite end, a **bear market**—when prices are steadily decreasing—is a riskier time to invest. But a lot of experts say you shouldn't look too closely at market trends. Because the market is volatile. Billionaire and business GOAT Warren Buffett once said, "If you aren't willing to own a stock for 10 years, don't even think about owning it for 10 minutes." Here are some other stock market scenarios.

For when there's a new stock on the block . . .

Hear the bells? That's the sign of an **IPO,** or initial public offering. It's like a company's stock market debutante ball. It's the first sale of a stock by a company to the public. This is a big deal, because the price of the company's stock often serves as a benchmark for its success. Bells are rung. Headlines are made. If you're a new investor, it's a risky idea to buy stock that just IPO'd since it doesn't have a track record of success yet.

I'm coming out... I want the world to know

For when you're watching to see how a stock is performing . . .

You'll be checking out a stock exchange. **NASDAQ** and the **New York Stock Exchange (NYSE)** are the two largest ones. When a company decides to offer an IPO, they'll typically choose one of these to host the party. NASDAQ is known for hosting a lot of tech stocks, while NYSE is known for hosting stocks from large companies with a stable record. These are known as blue-chip stocks and their name comes from blue gambling chips, the highest value chips used in casinos. *Viva las markets.*

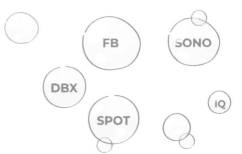

For when you want to check the stock market like you check the weather . . .

Take a look at a stock index. The **Dow Jones Industrial Average** is the best-known stock index in the US. Think of it like the music charts but for stocks. It's a list of 30 big-name stocks traded on either the NYSE or the NASDAQ. The index changes depending on how companies are performing. The list usually includes Apple, McDonald's, Nike, and Visa. It's also price-weighted, meaning that stocks with higher prices are given more importance when calculating the overall average. Insert Texas Instruments calculator here. The **S&P 500** is another well-known stock index. The biggest difference between this and the Dow is that the S&P includes more companies. So while the Dow is more standard, the S&P is more all-encompassing.

What's a smart investment strategy?

We can't tell you what exactly to invest in. Because the markets are moody. And we're not legally allowed to do that. But we can tell you some of the best things to keep in mind while investing. Note: You can and should try them all.

For the person who never wears the same outfit in a week . . .

Bring that diversification to your portfolio. Make sure you're invested in different places—it's less risky than putting all your eggs in one basket. Because if that one basket breaks, there will be a lot of yolks on your face. This is why mutual funds or ETFs are a popular option. It's like buying a collection of stocks and bonds instead of picking them individually yourself.

For the person who eats the same thing for breakfast every day . . .

Being a creature of habit is a good thing when it comes to investing. Decide to invest a certain amount of money each month and stick to it. Consider setting up automatic deposits to your investment funds.

For the person who likes to act fast . . .

Beware of **day trading.** This means you're buying and selling within the same day before the close of the markets. Generally not a good idea unless you have a LOT of experience.

that escalated quickly

For the person who paints their face at football games . . .

Being a fan on the sidelines is fine. But when you're investing, you're a player. Don't be a stock fan. Meaning don't buy Apple stock just because you really, really love your iPhone. If you're so passionate about your iPhone that you've been following its stock for years and understand what you're signing up for, that's a different story.

For when you're worried about paying rent . . .

Keep things separate. As in, don't invest the money you saved for your "need it" expenses. One of your biggest risks in investing is needing that money back ASAP. Like wine, you want to drink (sell) your stock once it's mature. If you'll need that money in three to five years, maybe don't invest it. Make sure you have other liquid funds, aka cash, available to you if you need it. This is where your emergency fund comes in.

For when you're wondering how to allocate your investment money . . .

Try the **120 rule.** Here's how it works: 120 minus your age is the percentage of your portfolio you should have in stocks. So if you're 25, 95 percent of your money should be in stocks while 5 percent should be in safer investments like bonds. When you buy ETFs or mutual funds, your portfolio mix should look something like that. The idea here is that the younger you are, the more risk you can take. The older (and the closer to retirement) you are, the less risk you want to take with your cash money. Investing in a target-date or "lifecycle" mutual fund in your 401(k) is the easiest way to make sure your risk level and asset allocation are right for you.

theSkimm: Investing is a way to make your money grow without having to earn more of it. It's a no-brainer. But it's important to put brains (yours or an advisor's) toward figuring out which investments work best for you.

Things That Are
Tedious

theSkimm on Taxes

It's taxing. Literally.

Filing your taxes is one of those semi-painful things that you just have to get done. It's less painful if you know what exactly you're filling out and how to avoid effing it up.

What dates do I need to know?

Ready, set, mark your calendars. There are some big dates to circle.

April 15-ish: The Big One. Usually. Tax Day almost always falls on the 15th. Key word: almost. Sometimes it shifts a day or two based on holiday and weekend timing. So make sure to double-check the date. This is the last day to file your tax return. If you need to hit snooze, file an extension by this day. This is also the last day to get as much as you can into an IRA (reminder: a way to save for retirement). If you're self-employed, today's the day you have to pay the government your first round of estimated taxes for the year.

June 15-ish, September 15-ish, January 15-ish: If you're self-employed or doing contract work, mark these days in your cal in addition to April 15. Not so fun fact: You have to pay the government (both the IRS and the state you're working in) estimated taxes every quarter.

> **Thing to know**
> An extension is an extension on how much time you have to file, not how much time you have to pay. You still need to submit an estimated payment by April 15 no matter what.

October 15: Oh hey, procrastinators. You knew this day was coming. If you asked for a six-month extension to file your tax return, here we are.

How should I get organized?

Starting in January every year, keep an email folder or a physical folder (if you're old-school) with all of your receipts that may qualify for itemized deductions. We'll get to the breakdown of all of those. But know you'll want to save things like charitable donations, tuition expenses, mortgage statements, and child care bills. Save the receipts to the folder in real time so when tax season rolls around, everything is already in one place.

file this under: old school

When should I start getting my tax forms together?

Experts say ASAP. But we know that we're all busy keeping and breaking our resolutions all of January, so we say start gathering it all in late February.

Speaking of forms . . . which ones should I start with?

Fine form. Here are the first two that should be on your radar.

For when you're starting a new full-time job . . .

W-4 the win. This is the form you fill out when you start a job so your employer knows how much to withhold from your paycheck for federal and state taxes. Your employer will have it on file. You'll be asked to fill out how many allowances you want to claim. Putting one or zero is really personal preference. If you claim zero, more taxes will be withheld per paycheck but you'll likely get more of a refund after you file your taxes. If you claim one or more allowances, you'll send less to the gov with each paycheck, but may have to pay more later on. Procrastinator's delight.

For when tax season's coming up . . .

Easy as 1, **W-2,** 3. This is the form that shows how much of your paycheck your company withheld to send in estimated taxes to the government. You should have gotten a copy in the mail in January. If you can't find it, ask your company to send you another one. Or check to see if you're set up to receive it digitally. You're going to need to reference this when filing your return. Note: If you switched jobs during the year, you'll need a W-2 from each company you worked at.

OK, it's crunch time. Which forms do I need to actually file?

Depends who you are. Here's how different people should get in fine form.

For when you have a full-time job . . .

You'll need a **1040.** Aka the long one or the individual tax return. This is the form where you put down what you made that year and some details about your personal situation. That helps you and the gov settle who needs to Venmo whom. And how much. *Psst* . . . if you talk to anyone about this, call it a "ten forty," not a "one oh four oh."

For when you freelance or have a side hustle . . .

Look out for a **1099.** Whoever is paying you during the year may send you one. It's kind of like a W-2, minus the withheld taxes. So you may need to pay taxes on it when you file your return. But you can reduce this income by claiming expenses you incurred along the way. For example, if you freelance in entertainment, you may be able to deduct the cost of Netflix or Hulu. Same for a news subscription if you do contract work at a media company. File it all under "research." Brb, need to binge some research.

Also, you may get other 1099s for interest on investments or dividends, aka a portion of a company's earnings that is paid to shareholders, or people that own that company's stock. *Psst* . . . say "ten ninety-nine" instead of "one oh nine nine."

For when you like to leave things to the last minute . . .

If you need an extension, you'll need to fill out a **4868.** This is basically your permission slip to take your time. Remember: You have until October (usually October 15) to get it done. Circle that date on your calendar.

I have all my forms. Now what?

Fill out the 1040 and send it off. There are a couple of ways to do that: by mail, on the IRS website, through sites and apps like TurboTax and H&R Block, or—if you decide you want more help—an accountant can take care of it.

Do I need an accountant, or can I do this myself?

Accountants can be really helpful. But also expensive. It comes down to how complex your money situation is. Do you own your own biz? Own a property? If so, you might want to consider an accountant to help make sure nothing falls through the cracks. If not, there's software out there to help you prep your returns and file.

Wait, back up. How do I even read this thing?

Slowly. There are a few sections of your 1040 that you should mentally highlight.

Income and personal info section

Where you fill out who you are and how much you made the past year. This part is the most straightforward.

Deductions section

Where the gov lowers your taxable income based on your status or specific expenses you paid during the year.

Tax credits section

Where the amount you owe the gov is reduced by certain credits.

How do I make sure I get the biggest discount?

First things first: Don't lie. But make sure you get everything you're qualified for. This is where exemptions and deductions come in. **Exemptions** are tax discounts you can get right off the bat for just being you. You can get more by having plus-ones you're responsible for, aka dependents. That includes kids, or parents or grandparents you're taking care of. If you're declaring someone as a dependent, you're going to need his or her Social Security number or ITIN (Individual Taxpayer Identification Number). Make sure you have this info.

Whatever your filing status is on the last day of the year is your status for the entire year. So, if you're not yet married on the last day of the year, you can't use a married filing status—even if you get married early the next year before you file your tax return. The same is true of children that may qualify you for tax benefits. If you're having a baby in the winter, cross your fingers that you're changing diapers by December so you can claim those child-related benefits (like the Child Tax Credit) for the entire year.

What about deductions?

Deductions get a bit more complicated. There are two kinds: standard and itemized. Here's the difference.

Standard deduction

The prix fixe of taxes. You get a flat-rate reduction of your taxable income based on your filing status. There are five different types of statuses: 1) Single, 2) Married Filing Jointly, 3) Married Filing Separately, 4) Head of Household (fancy way to say single parent or someone caring for an adult) and 5) Qualifying Widow(er). If you choose to go the standard route, you'll pick your status and get a, yup, standard discount based on your choice. Pros: Simple, no extra work, and the IRS pinkie promises not to ask for all your receipts if they audit you. Cons: Depending on your situation, you could be missing out on itemized deductions that save you cash money.

Standard Deduction

Single

Married Filing Separately

Married Filing Jointly

Head of Household

Qualifying Widow(er)

$ $ $

Itemized

The à la carte of taxes. This is trying to pick up *alllll* the deductions you can. You get 'em for a wide range of things like giving to charity, large medical expenses, mortgage interest, real estate taxes on your home, or state income taxes (usually paid through your W-2). If you do the math, and the itemized deductions are more than the standard deduction, you could end up saving dollar bills.

ITEMIZED

Charitable Donations $$
Large Medical Expenses $$
Mortgage Interest $$
Real Estate Taxes
on Your Home $$
State Income Taxes $$

What are some itemized deductions I should look out for?

Medical

Beginning in 2019 you can deduct medical expenses that exceed 10 percent of your adjusted gross income. So if your adjusted gross income is $50,000 and you spent $5,500 in medical expenses during the year, you could deduct $500 ($50,000 x 0.1 = $5,000). So that $500 leftover is the amount that exceeds 10 percent.

Interest

Mortgage interest is deductible for home loans up to $750,000.

Charitable donations

If you've given to charity you can deduct that amount (up to 50 percent of your income). Paying it forward pays off.

Home office deductions

If you WFH, you can claim some special deductions. Because the tax code loves to be confusing, the rate is $5 per square foot for up to three hundred square feet of space. But if you use this space as a bedroom or child care room slash office you can't claim it. It has to be your primary office.

State income taxes

If you pay taxes to the state on your income, that can be a deduction on your federal taxes. If you pay the state property taxes for things like real estate, you can deduct that as well. In total you can deduct up to $10,000.

Casualty, disaster, and theft losses

These can be deductible if the president declares a federal disaster in your area.

What about credits?

In school and in life, extra credit always wins. Tax credits are actually better than deductions. Instead of a reduction of your taxable income, they're an actual dollar-for-dollar reduction of the amount you owe. Here are a few of the credits to look out for:

Child tax credit

Oh, baby. This is the most common credit used, and you can get up to $2,000 shaved off your taxes for each child.

Education credit

This is called the American Opportunity Tax Credit, and if you're a college student you should take it. It can save you up to $2,500. A+.

Electric vehicle credit

If you're living that hybrid life, you may be able to get a credit for $2,000 to $7,500.

I'm married. What does this mean for me?

You can live joint filingly ever after. We'll get to what that means. If you and your SO got hitched before the end of the last tax year, you have two options. You can file together (joint) or solo (separate).

Joint

When two become one. And you pool your money together. Income minus deductions (standard or itemized) equals your collective taxable income. That puts you in a certain tax bracket. People filing together have different bracket thresholds than single filers. Pros: Joint filers can often get a better deal (aka higher deduction) just for being married.

Separate

Shout out to those going it alone. Even if you're married, filing separately could be a way to save some cash . . . sometimes. Like if one of you has high medical expenses. The rules get tricky, and it depends on your personal situation, so look into it if you think there's a chance you could save.

How do I make sure I don't eff it up?

There are mistakes and then there are mistakes that cost you money. Everyone will tell you to spell-check and get your Social Security number right. Here are some less obvious mistakes to avoid.

For when you feel like you forgot something . . .

Make sure it's not Tax Day. Circle April 15 (or whatever day it is that year) in your calendar. If you file late, you will pay the price. The penalty is usually 5 percent of the unpaid taxes for each month that a return is late. It starts the day after the tax filing due date and won't go over 25 percent. You'll get a separate bill for that.

For when you don't like "labels" . . .

You're going to have to like them here. Make sure to choose the correct filing status, out of the five listed earlier. There are a lot of people who choose the wrong status and end up getting less juice out of their tax refund.

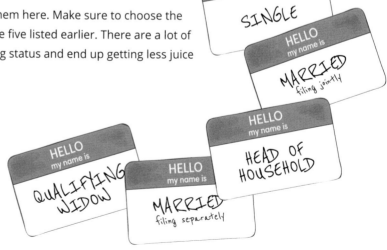

For when you have a missed call . . .

It won't be from the IRS. Beware of scam calls. They happen more often than you think, and seem legit. The callers may know a lot of your info and usually make it so that "IRS" pops up on caller ID. The IRS will never call you asking for an immediate payment or threatening to have you arrested. Just hang up and call the IRS directly at 1-800-829-1040. Or email them at phishing@irs.gov.

For when you want to finish strong . . .

Sign on the dotted line. If you're filing your taxes old-school, on paper, you need to sign. If you're doing everything online, you'll be asked for your Identity Protection Personal Identification Number, aka an **IP PIN.** This is like two-step verification to make sure no one's using your Social Security number and to protect you from identity theft. If you filled out last year's taxes, check that return to find this number. If you don't know what yours is, ping the IRS.

Greeting	Edit

Voicemail

1-800-IRS
Wire us money plz

1-800-FRAUD
Gimme gimme cash

911-NOFUN
Here to rob you

1-866-RUN
You owe us

1-800-SOS
I'm trying to trick you

Any other tips to save cash money?

Avoid short-term **capital gains** taxes. Capital gains are the profits from the sale of an asset. That includes shares of stock, a piece of land, a business, a home. They're considered taxable income and are taxed at the same rate as ordinary income. If you hold on to the asset for more than a year before selling, they're considered long-term capital gains and may qualify for a reduced tax rate.

Does everyone have to file taxes?

Nope. If you make below a certain amount (for example, $12,000 if you're under 65 and single), you get a pass. But you still may be eligible for tax refunds and credits, so it's up to you if you wanna get in on the Tax Day spirit.

Do I get a reward for doing all this?

Yes. Sometimes. But it's not always a good thing. If you get a big tax refund, it probably means you've been paying Uncle Sam too much throughout the year—and basically giving him an interest-free loan. The amount you get back will depend on how much you had withheld from your paycheck. (Remember when you filled out that W-4?) The IRS issues you this cash money back 21 days after it gets your tax forms. Set up a direct deposit for your tax refund. You'll get it much faster than waiting for a check.

theSkimm: No one said doing your taxes was fun. But you'll feel better when it's over. Mark your calendars and get your forms in order. You got this.

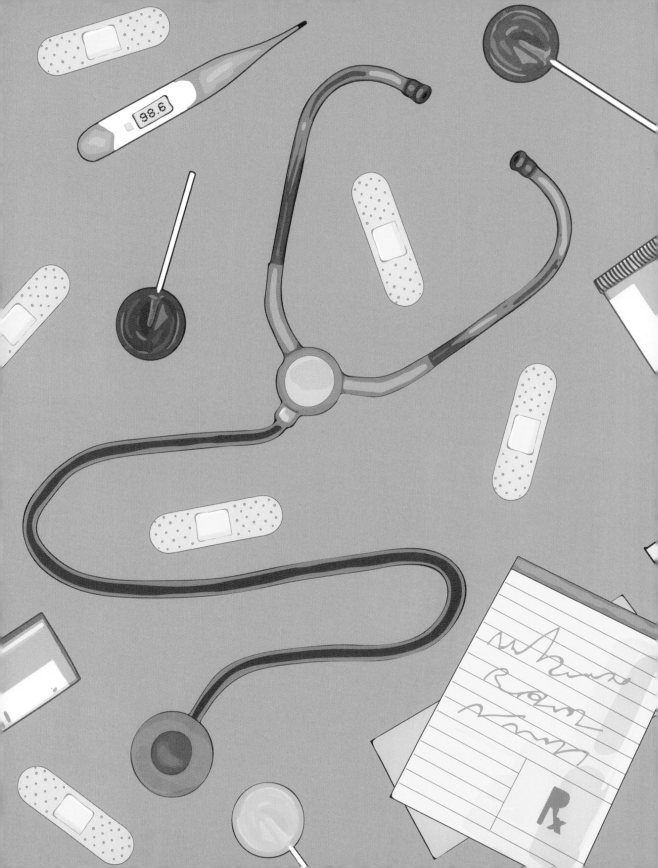

Things
No One Really Understands

theSkimm on Health Insurance

The sure part of insurance feels elusive.

How can you be sure you're not getting ripped off? How can you be sure you chose the best plan? The one thing you *can* be sure of is that everyone has a lot of questions about health insurance.

How do health insurance companies make money?

From customers paying monthly premiums. A health plan is a contract between you and an insurance company. It says that the insurance company will pay a portion of your medical bills, bills, bills if you get sick or hurt. To keep your plan, you pay your insurance company a certain amount every month. That's called a **premium.** The insurance company keeps that cash on hand to pay all or some of the bill when customers get sick.

Because insurance companies have all the customers, they can negotiate prices with doctors and hospital systems. The ones they have deals with are **in-network,** so the patient will end up with a smaller tab at the end of it. All the others are **out-of-network,** aka you're basically on the hook for most or all of the bill.

Can you pay my bills
Can you pay my telephone bills
Can you pay my automo-bills

How do I get a plan?

Depends on your personal situation.

If you're employed full-time . . .

Usually through work. If you have a nine-to-five (or -six or -seven) your employer will likely pay all or a portion of your premium, and the rest will be taken out of your paycheck every month. Legally, a "large company" (50 or more employees) is required to pay a portion of your insurance.

Workin' 9 to 5
What a way to make a livin'
Barely gettin' by
It's all takin' and no givin'

If you're unemployed or self-employed . . .

Through a government exchange. These are mostly run by the federal government, but some states have their own marketplaces. This means the government acts like your employer and negotiates deals with providers. Visit HealthCare.gov to check out plans. There's also **Medicare** for people over 65 and **Medicaid** for people whose salary is under a certain amount. These are low-cost plans that are partially paid for by the government.

Get down, get down, get down,
Get down, get down tonight, baby
Get down, get down, get down

If you're under 26 . . .

If your family has a health insurance plan, you can stay on it. For now. If you're about to turn 26—one, we are jealous. Two, take the time to enroll in your employer's plan or a marketplace plan. Because of your impending birthday, you can do this even if it's not during an **open enrollment** period.

What's my age again?
What's my age again?

Open enrollment . . . when's that again?

If you're going the marketplace route, aka through HealthCare.gov, open enrollment generally starts in early November and goes through mid-December. If you're going through your employer's plan, it varies. Insert reminder to email HR. You can enroll at any time if you experience a "qualifying life event." Sounds scary, but it often involves popping bottles. Getting married, moving, having a kid, and leaving your job all qualify.

Celebrate good times, come on!
(Let's celebrate)
Celebrate good times, come on!
(Let's celebrate)

How much does a plan cost?

Also depends. Sensing a pattern? On top of your monthly premium, there are other things you pay too. Fun times. Here's a checklist of the medical payments you'll generally have to make, what they mean, and why you care.

☑ Premium

The one we've talked about. This is your monthly fee for getting insurance. All health plans have premiums, but some are higher than others.

☑ Deductible

The amount you have to pay toward your medical costs before your insurance company starts picking up part of the bill. So if your deductible is $2,500, you're on the hook for that much—on top of the premiums you've already paid. Then insurance raises its hand.

☑ Co-pay

The flat fee you pay for covered medical services after you've met your deductible. Like a cover charge without the open bar. Preventive care, like annual physicals, may be fully covered by insurance (meaning no co-pay).

Thing to know
Out-of-pocket max. The limit does exist. It's the most you'll pay during your coverage period (typically twelve months). If your out-of-pocket max is $6,000, you will never have to pay over that amount during the year of your benefits coverage.

☑ Co-insurance

Once you hit your deductible, you still have to pay a certain percentage of your medical bills. So let's say your coinsurance is 20 percent. Once you hit your deductible, a $100 doctor's bill will now cost only $20.

These aren't just definitions in a tedious dictionary. It's important to know the difference between these things because you want to take into account *allll* the costs that come along with staying healthy. Generally, plans with lower monthly premiums have higher deductibles, and plans with higher premiums have lower deductibles. So don't get immediate heart eyes at a low-premium plan.

Ultimately, your bill will depend on your age, where you live, and your plan. But to give you an idea, in a year, the average costs for a single person to pay for a year of healthcare range from $6,000 to $10,000.

Gimme some plan types.

Sing it all together now: H to the MO. The two main plan types you'll see are **HMO** and **PPO.** Here are the differences between them and why you might want to choose one over the other.

For when you're the monogamous type . . .

Consider putting a ring on an **HMO.** This pays only for healthcare that's in-network, aka hospitals that insurance providers have negotiated deals with. Premiums tend to be lower, but these plans require you to get a referral from your primary care physician (PCP) to see a specialist. If you're not picky and want to pay less monthly, this might be for you.

For when you're the playing-the-field type . . .

Consider going for a **PPO.** This covers care that's both in- and out-of-network. But for all these options, you'll pay a higher monthly premium. And you still end up paying more for out-of-network care than in-network care. So if you want more fish in the healthcare sea, but don't mind paying up, this might be for you.

I think you're sea sick

This all sounds expensive. Gimme some tips to save . . .

There are savings accounts for that. Specific savings accounts. **Health savings accounts (HSAs)** and **flexible savings accounts (FSAs)** are savings accounts specifically for your health insurance plans. You can contribute pre-tax dollars to them to save and pay for things like pricey deductibles, co-pays, and prescriptions. The biggest difference between them? With an HSA, any money you don't use in the account rolls over to the next year. But to be able to qualify for an HSA, you need to have a high-deductible health plan (at least $1,350). If you have the option, it's a safer bet since the money rolls over regardless of whether you use it that year. With an FSA, there's no eligibility requirement but it is "use it or lose it"— meaning you'll have to say "bye" to any unused balance. But there are two options your plan may have: a $500 flat rollover or a two-and-a-half-month grace period to spend the remainder of the funds. Saving (money) grace. Pro tip: Amazon has a page of FSA or HSA eligible items.

I just lost my job. What do I do?

You have **COBRA** to help in the short-term. COBRA stands for Consolidated Omnibus Budget Reconciliation Act. Translation: It's a federal law that may let you keep your health insurance after you lose your full-time job. The catch? It's only for a limited time (usually 18 months). It's for full-time employees (that is, it doesn't apply to freelancers who lose a client). But the biggest drawback to COBRA is that you have to pay the full cost of the premium, when your employer paid all or a portion of it before. This also applies to divorce if you were on your partner's plan.

Because COBRA can get pricey, experts recommend that you also look into marketplace plans. Losing your job is considered a qualifying event, so you can enroll at any time.

Am I covered even if I'm OOO for a medical reason?

Whether you had a baby, got sick, or are taking care of a family member, you may be able to take some much-needed time and stay covered. But it depends on where you live and what your plan is. On the federal level, all employees working at "large companies" (50 or more) are allowed 12 weeks of protected leave for these medical reasons. The catch? The leave doesn't have to be paid. So many people can't afford to take it.

Individual states have been enacting their own laws to make this better for employees. New York, California, New Jersey, Rhode Island, and Washington all have paid-family-leave policies. And a company's insurance plan may come with its own paid leave policy (which is usually better than the federal requirement).

What about fertility coverage?

If you're going through fertility treatments, like IVF, there's a chance part of it's covered. If you work full-time and get insurance through your job, your HR department can elect to provide this. Contact HR (your favorite thing to hear) to see if your plan covers you.

When it comes to egg freezing, most plans do not cover it. But that appears to be changing. A growing number of tech companies now cover the procedure. And if you have a diagnosed fertility problem, you may be able to get egg freezing covered.

If you're on a marketplace plan, your fertility coverage depends on the state you live in. Massachusetts, Maryland, Connecticut, Rhode Island, Arkansas, California, Hawaii, Illinois, Louisiana, Montana, New Jersey, New York, Ohio, Texas, and West Virginia all offer some form of coverage. But it's not a federal rule to cover this type of treatment.

How do I file an insurance claim?

The easiest way to do this is to have your medical services provider (reception at your doc's office) submit the claim electronically. But if your doc is out-of-network, you might have to file the claim yourself. Contact your insurance company or visit their website to receive the claim form. You'll need things like your insurance policy number, group plan number, and reasons for the service.

What should I do if the claim gets denied?

Contact your insurance company. The info should be on the back of your insurance card and on the denial letter. And come to the call prepared. Bring a list of Qs about the denial, and gather documents like your policy, the summary of benefits and coverage, and that denial letter. Your claim may have been denied because of a simple error, and it's worth fighting for that payment.

Do I really need insurance?

With the rising cost of healthcare, a growing number of people have been saying "Thanks but no thanks" and opting out of insurance. About one in five Americans reportedly do not have insurance. This may seem attractive in the short term, as less money will be taken out of your monthly paycheck. But if something unforeseen happens and you need treatment, you could end up paying *wayyy* more than those monthly payments would add up to.

Why is healthcare in the US so confusing?

That's another full-length book. Healthcare is extremely expensive, and politicians are extremely divided on how the country should handle it. One thing you hear a lot about is **"Medicare-for-all"** or a "single-payer system." That's what Canada has. It means the federal government takes care of everyone's bill. Team pro-single-payer says it will provide healthcare for the largest number of Americans and streamline the complicated system. Team anti-single-payer says it will hike taxes way up for Americans and make people wait in long lines for care.

theSkimm: Health insurance has an unhealthy amount of confusion surrounding it. But regardless of your opinion on how it should be handled, you need to know what you're signing up for.

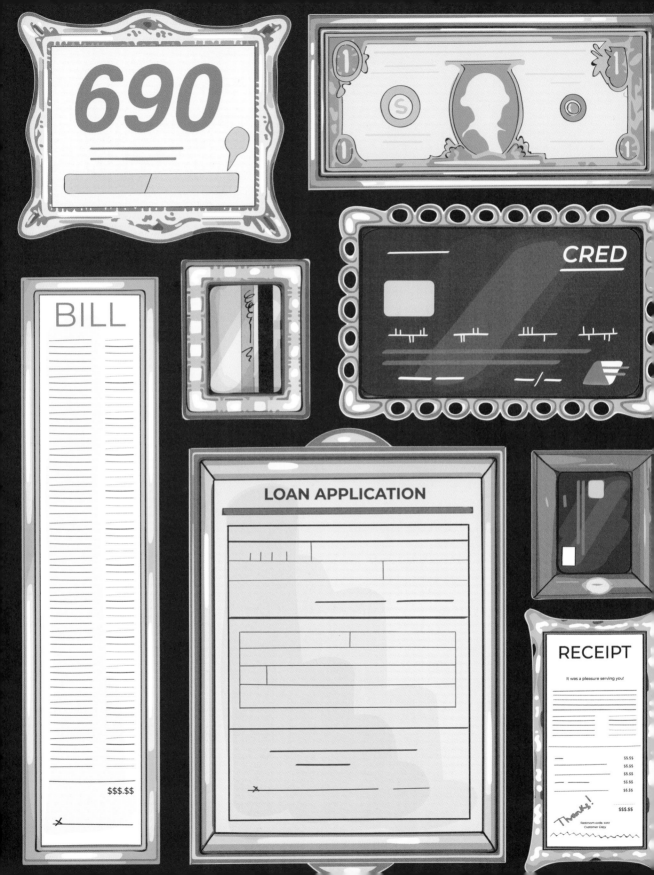

Things with a *Reputation*

theSkimm on Credit

If a picture's worth a thousand words, a credit score is worth . . . more than that.

It's tangible proof of your financial trustworthiness. It's used by banks to determine whether or not to give you money, and it determines whether you get the best interest rates on loans and insurance policies.

Back up . . . what exactly is a credit score?

Think of it like your personal Uber rating. But there's more at stake than a bad ride. A credit score is a snapshot of your financial history—whether you make payments on time, whether you max out your cards, how much debt you're in, and more.

How do I check my credit score?

Once a year, you can get it for free from AnnualCreditReport.com. That's actually a site. But some credit card issuers also now offer it for free at any time of year, so check if yours is one of them. You'll also see your credit score referred to as a **FICO score**. This stands for the Fair Isaac Corporation, the company whose software calculates your credit score. Experts recommend that you check it at least once a year.

Who decides my credit score?

Ultimately you. There are three credit reporting agencies: Equifax, Experian, and Transunion. Think of them like the test graders. And like teachers, they each might give out points a little differently. You should request a report from each of the three credit reporting agencies so you can see the differences and check for inaccuracies (more on that later).

How do I know if I passed?

Credit scores are on a scale from 300 to 850: 300 is very bad; 850 is very good. Here's how everything in between stacks up.

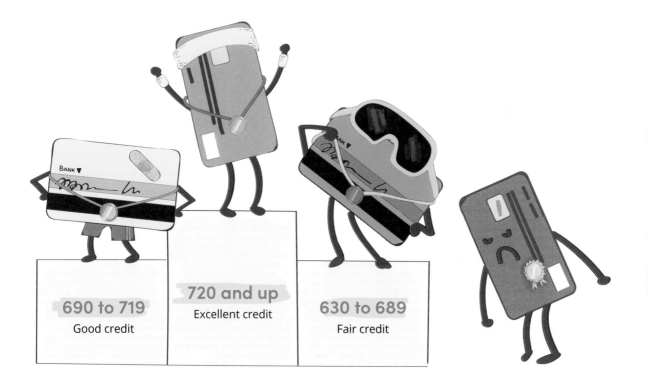

690 to 719
Good credit

720 and up
Excellent credit

630 to 689
Fair credit

300 to 629
Bad credit

How exactly is my score calculated?

There are a bunch of things that hurt and help your credit score. Here are all the pieces of the credit pie.

Payment history: 35 percent

Paying your credit card bill and loan payments on time is the most important thing for good credit. A payment that is 30 days late can cost someone with a credit score of 780 or higher (hi, overachiever) anywhere from 90 to 110 points.

Credit utilization: 30 percent

This is the ratio of how much you owe to how much you're allowed to spend. Every time you pay with plastic, you're utilizing your credit. So if you owe $200 and your spending limit is $1,000, then your credit utilization is . . . drumroll please . . . 20 percent. You want to keep this low.

Length of history: 15 percent

Longer credit history increases your score, since it shows the bank you have a proven track record.

Credit mix: 10 percent

This is how many types of credit you have in use. The more you have, the more data points the bank has to judge you. This is a good thing if you make all your payments on time and a bad thing if you don't.

Account inquiries and new credit: 10 percent

If you're opening up a bunch of new cards in a short period of time, it's a bad look. If a lender looks at your credit report you also get a slight penalty.

Why do I get penalized for someone looking at my report?

It depends who's looking. A **hard inquiry** and a **soft inquiry** are two different things. A hard inquiry is when a lender checks specifically to approve a new credit card or a loan (home and auto included). A soft inquiry is when a potential employer does a background check. A hard inquiry will affect your credit score, while a soft inquiry won't. Hard-knock life.

OK, so . . . how do I improve my credit?

Aside from the obvious "Pay your credit cards on time," there are some other ways you can improve your score.

For when something looks off in your credit report . . .

Dispute it. A lot of people have errors on their credit report that they never take a red pen to. This may include a payment that you actually paid on time. Or, more commonly, a very old payment. If you miss a payment and it lowers your credit score, that's only allowed to stay on your report for seven years. Credit card bills and student loan payments included. Meaning if it's still there, you can get it removed so it no longer affects your credit. You can file this dispute online with your credit bureau (reminder: Experian, Equifax, or Transunion).

For when your credit utilization is high . . .

Make multiple small payments all month instead of one big lump sum at the end, to keep your balance down. Or you can call your credit card company and ask them to raise your spending limit. Make sure to ask if you can do this without a hard inquiry into your credit.

What about my SO's score?

When you get married, you keep an individual credit score. But if you're applying for a loan with someone—a spouse or long-term partner—both of your scores will be evaluated. And if your partner's score is low, it'll hurt your chances.

theSkimm: Age is just a number, but credit is a number that affects your ability to buy a home or car and move on to different stages in life. Get it in check before taking big steps.

MORTGAGE

Things That Are
Yours

theSkimm on Leasing and Ownership

Saying "mine" to a house and a car might seem far away.

Or you might already be actively planning for it. Whether you're renting, buying, driving, or none of the above, there are some things you should know when it's time to move on up.

First things first . . . renters insurance.

Because training wheels. Even if you're not ready to buy, chances are you're renting an apartment or house. You'll want renters insurance to go with that. No, this doesn't just come with your apartment. Your landlord's insurance (for damages to the building) doesn't extend to your stuff. You'll need to get your own policy if you haven't already.

What does renters insurance cover?

Renters insurance has your back in case of things like fire, theft, and flooding and makes it so that you don't have to pay for all the damages. Many plans also have **liability coverage**—meaning coverage that protects you if you're sued. For example, if a guest falls down your stairs or your dog bites someone in your apartment, you may be legally liable. Woof.

How do I get renters insurance

'cause I know that I'm delicate (delicate)

Do your research

Look into policies at companies like Allstate, AAA, GEICO, and Lemonade. The value of your belongings may impact the amount you pay for a renters insurance policy (the higher in value, the more you pay). Also, if you already have car insurance (more on that later), see if that company also offers renters insurance. You may get a discount for bundling your policies. And consider upgrading your home to get a lower rate. If you update your locks or install an alarm system, this can make you pay less in the long term.

Stalk your space

Take an inventory of every item in your space, including electronics, art, home goods, clothing, and kitchenware. Estimate their value. Hint: Not what you paid for them, but what they are worth now. This is how you'll approximate how much insurance you'll need. Try to make as close of a guesstimate as you can.

Get a quote

Contact some insurance companies for (usually free) quotes.

FRAGILE

DO YOUR RESEARCH

STALK YOUR SPACE

GET A QUOTE

How much does renters insurance cost?

A typical plan costs between $5 and $15 a month. So around what you pay to stream music and movies. Worth it.

Moving on up . . . to home ownership. When should I buy a house?

Most people say you should consider buying only if you're going to be in the place for five years or more. More importantly, you need to be financially ready. While it seems crazy to put down that much cash money, remember that you don't have to pay the full cost of the house up front. Enter: mortgages.

What do I need to know about mortgages?

A mortgage is really just a number. A VIP number that will dictate how you plan financially.

Pretty much everyone who buys a house has a mortgage. It's a big loan to help you swipe right on that new property. Your house then works as collateral on the loan. If you can't pay off your mortgage, the bank can take back your house. This process is known as **foreclosure** or "something to avoid."

How much is a mortgage loan?

Typically, 80 percent of the cost of the house. So a lot. You have to pay back the loan, plus interest, over a set period of time (usually thirty years).

So how do I qualify for a mortgage?

The bank needs to trust you to repay your loan. So you'll need to have enough money for the bank to pick you, choose you, love you. Here are some of the steps to take in the years leading up to home ownership.

Give credit where credit's due

As in, improve your credit score. Credit is one of the most important things a bank looks at. Generally, if your credit score is under 600, you won't get a loan. And lenders (banks) typically reserve the lowest interest rate payments for people with a credit score of 760 or above. Get your credit score up by doing things like making credit card and bill payments on time. See: the credit section you just read.

Feng shui your finances

Save, save, save now so you can afford a home later. If you can't pay at least 10 percent of the home's worth (ideally 20 percent), you probably aren't ready to buy that house. Other costs you'll need to save for: monthly payments, property taxes, homeowners insurance, costs of repairs, and maintenance of the home, particularly if you're buying an old house. Because haunted houses can also be haunted by higher bills.

Seek (pre)approval

You'll want to get preapproved by the bank before you start shopping for houses. This is like a parental permission slip to attend a field trip (the field trip is your house). It'll show real estate agents and sellers that you're serious and in good financial health, and give you an edge in the buying process. Here's some of what you'll need: tax forms, bank statements, Social Security number, and maybe more depending on the lender. All of this is to prove you're a living, breathing, money-making human who can be trusted to pay back a mortgage once you close on the house.

Let's talk about that whole "paying back" process . . .

You have to pay back the **principal** (amount of the loan) plus interest (a certain percentage every year). If your loan's due back over 30 years, it might seem to make the most sense to divide your loan amount by 30 and pay that dollar amount every year. But the way it normally works is that you pay more as you start to make more. So you'll pay a little bit more every year, with the assumption that you'll make more money as you move up in your career.

For when you like consistency . . .

Get your fix. As in, look into a **fixed-rate loan**. This is the most common type of home loan. You'll pay the same rate of interest every year.

For when you like to follow trends . . .

Stay adjusted. As in, look into an **adjustable rate mortgage (ARM)**. These loans have a lower initial interest rate that adjusts or resets every year depending on the markets. So you may start by paying 5 percent interest the first year but pay higher the next year due to the Fed raising interest rates.

For when you want to sell the house before your mortgage is paid off . . .

The mortgage doesn't go away. You still have to pay it back. Most people use some of the money they make from selling the house to pay off the rest of their mortgage.

amount owed

amount paid

For if you think you're going to sell the house kinda soon . . .

Get yourself a mortgage that pops. As in, look into a **balloon mortgage.** This works like a fixed-rate mortgage but then has a lump-sum payment due at the end to make up for all those years you won't be repaying on a schedule. This is considered risky, since you're effed if you can't pay that lump sum when you sell.

I just want to know how to save money.

Got it. All of this depends on your financial situation, but in general . . . if you can pay off your mortgage early, you'll save money. Because you won't have to pay that interest every year.

OK, ready to *park* myself at this house for a while. Let's talk cars.

Car ownership isn't for everyone. You might be uber enthusiastic about ride-sharing or live in a city where public transportation's the best option. While car ownership on the whole hasn't been declining, it's been going down amongst millennials. If you still think you want a car, consider how much flexibility you need. Do you need to take a car to work every day? Do you travel locally on the weekends? If you answered yes to both of those questions (and you have good credit and a healthy savings account) you might want to consider revving up to buy a car.

Can I take out a loan?

Yup. Many of the lenders for mortgage loans also deal in auto loans. But know that a car is a **depreciating asset,** à la milk, whereas a house is hopefully an **appreciating asset,** à la red wine. Meaning the value of your car will consistently go down as new models are released, while the value of your house will hopefully go up with the real estate market and improvements you make to it. Taking out an auto loan means you're paying yearly interest on something whose resale value keeps going down. The cure? Either pay in cash . . . or, if you don't have a casual 30K lying around, negotiate for good terms on your auto loan. That might mean getting the lender to pay for some added fees or doing comparison shopping and finding better rates from other lenders. Good credit gives you leverage here.

You also might want to consider leasing a car instead of buying one. A lot of the time, it means lower monthly payments compared to the loan terms for a car you purchased. That's because a lease takes the depreciation of a car into account.

How much should I expect to pay for a car?

Depends on your wheels. A typical midsize car will set you back about $25,000, while a midsize SUV will be about $31,000. And a midsize luxury car will go for about $55,000.

How do I make sure I don't get ripped off?

First, check the mileage. Any new car you're buying should have less than 10 miles on it. If you're buying a used car, know that 13,000 miles a year is considered average. So the average 10-year-old car should have around 130,000 miles on the odometer. Anything more than that and you may want to take a turn toward negotiating a lower price (or getting off the exit ramp and just not buying the car).

EXIT ↗
Adulthood

get in, loser, we're getting mortgages

theSkimm: Ownership is a sign of growing up. Don't panic; plan for it.

Skimm

THE
WORLD

In "Skimm the World," we'll get into historic global issues, movements, and relationships between countries. Then, we'll move to D.C. to see how the government of the most powerful country in the world functions, how elections really work, and how you can enact real change at the polls.

The news cycle moves quickly. Behind every headline's five minutes of fame, there's a lot of historical context. Most of it traces back to who gets along, who doesn't, and who owes who money. Tale as old as time.

Things That Make the
World Go Round
theSkimm on Geopolitics

It's not a small world after all.

Captain Planet is home to 7.5 billion people, an estimated 6,000 languages, and 4,200 religions . . . standing on top of 4.5 billion years of history.

First up . . . we'll set the stage with historical context, the movements, and international relationships that have shaped the world today.

Types of Governments

The "isms," the "chys," the "cy." Gang's all here. Here's a refresher on some types of government, political parties, and movements you hear about a lot.

Democracy

The "We, the people" type. It's a government run by the people, meaning majority rules. Today, more than half of the countries in the world are democracies. A lot of them—including the US—are representative democracies: You elect people, or representatives, to vote on issues for you. While democracy is considered the most free and, yes, democratic form of gov, the US has been criticized for forcefully trying to spread democracy worldwide.

Monarchy

The "Uneasy lies the head that wears a crown" type. In a monarchy, a single ruler has all the authority, and it's usually hereditary. Most monarchies that exist today are constitutional monarchies where the monarch can be considered a figurehead (like the UK). Then there are absolute monarchies, where the royals are also the heads of gov (like Saudi Arabia and Brunei).

Communism

The "Sharing is caring" type. All property and means of production are owned collectively. The aim? To create a classless society where everyone is truly equal. The result? Often mass poverty, in part because there are fewer incentives to succeed. It's the opposite of capitalism. China, North Korea, Vietnam, Laos, and Cuba are the last communist countries standing.

Socialism

The "communism, but make it less intense" type. Like communism, it's all about equality. Unlike communism, most socialists believe that workers can earn wages and spend that money however they choose, and the means of production are owned by the gov and shared by the people. But it's criticized for the same reasons as communism. Then there's democratic socialism, which you've been hearing about in recent years. It embraces a lot of basic socialist principles but also supports democratic ideals, like freedom of speech and free and fair elections.

Populism

The "power to the people" type. It's a political movement all about returning power to the people. These movements tend to be antiestablishment and full of working-class voters trying to take back control from the "out-of-touch elites." This one's been cropping up a lot in recent years.

Oligarchy

The "You can't sit with us" type. It's when a small group of people has control over everything. South Africa under apartheid was an example of an oligarchy.

World History 101

Get up close and personal with some of the biggest international events of the last hundred years or so. *This is not an exhaustive history.* What you're going to see? Events that you learned about in history class with a lasting global impact. What you're not going to see? More recent US-centric events (think: Watergate, Clinton-Lewinsky scandal).

Assassination of Archduke Franz Ferdinand

1914

One of the causes of World War I. Back then, Austria and Hungary were one kingdom (creatively called Austria-Hungary). Archduke Franz Ferdinand, who was set to inherit the throne, was assassinated by a Serbian nationalist. This made Austria-Hungary, with the backing of Germany, declare war on Serbia. Germany then declared war on Serbian ally Russia. Then France. Then Britain. *Aaand* WWI.

Armenian Genocide

1915–1916

The massacre of up to 1.5 million Armenians living in the Ottoman Empire (headquartered in modern-day Turkey) during WWI. Ottoman rulers, and many people living there, were Muslim. And many people discriminated against Armenian Christians. After WWI started, the Ottomans accused the Armenians of being traitors and began executing them and deporting them to concentration camps. Today, Turkey still objects to calling it a genocide and denies the scope of what happened.

Sykes-Picot Agreement

1916

A secret agreement between Britain and France that let the two countries say *mine* to Arab lands in the Ottoman Empire after

WWI (the Ottomans were on the side that went on to lose the war). The goal? Suppress Arab influence and increase European influence in the region.

Treaty of Versailles
1919

The end of WWI. This was the treaty that ended the war. The biggest takeaway? Germany had to foot the bill. It was agreed that since Germany had caused the war, it should pay for the damage (including homes and factories destroyed, ammo, uniforms, and more). The price tag was around $33 billion.

Third Reich
1933–45

The official name for the Nazi regime, active before and during World War II. The First Reich was the medieval Holy Roman Empire, which lasted until 1806. The Second Reich was the German Empire from 1871 to 1918.

Blitzkrieg
1933–45

A German term for "lightning war." This was a super-fast, concentrated attack the Germans used frequently to confuse their Allied opponents during World War II. Today, the word *blitz* in football comes from it.

Pearl Harbor
1941

The Japanese surprise attack on a US naval base in Hawaii. It killed more than 2,000 people and prompted the US's entry into WWII.

D-Day

1944

The beginning of the end of WWII. This is also called the Invasion of Normandy or that time more than 150,000 Allied soldiers made a surprise landing on German-occupied territory in northern France. The Battle of Normandy lasted for several months and more than 425,000 troops died.

D-Day Beaches

NORMANDY

Hiroshima and Nagasaki Bombings

1945

The US's atomic bombing of two Japanese cities, Hiroshima and Nagasaki, during WWII. The two bombings killed at least 200,000 people, almost entirely civilians. These are the only times nuclear weapons have been used in armed conflict. Ever.

Nuremberg Trials

1945–46

The trials of prominent Nazis after WWII ended. Judges from the Allied forces—the UK, France, the Soviet Union, and the US—held them. These top-ranking Nazis were charged with things like crimes against humanity and crimes against peace. 12 of them were sentenced to death.

Cold War

1947–91

The decades-long staring contest between the US and the **Soviet Union.** Even though the two countries fought together during WWII, things were tense. The US wasn't into the Soviets' communist government and aggressive leader (Joseph Stalin), while the Soviets resented the US's late entry into WWII. What happened there did not stay there: The conflict fueled multiple proxy wars. (Keep reading . . .)

Kashmir Conflict

1947–present

Before 1947, India and Pakistan were ruled by Britain. Then the Brits said "Cheerio" and gave both countries their independence. They were divided into the majority-Hindu India and the majority-Muslim Pakistan. But an area called Kashmir (pronounced like the sweater), was contested after India took control of it. So Pakistan invaded. Cue violence and the first war over the territory. China saw a power vacuum and snatched up part of Kashmir for itself, too. Now Kashmir is divided among India, Pakistan, and China. There have been three wars fought over this land. The conflict has killed nearly 50,000 people.

State of Israel Established

1948

In the late 19th century, Zionism gained more of a footing. Zionism: the nationalist movement of the Jewish people. It supports the reestablishment of a Jewish state in Israel. At the time, this land was part of British-controlled Palestine. Fast-forward to after the Holocaust—in which six million Jewish people were killed—and the case for a Jewish homeland became stronger than ever. In 1947, the UN said that the Jewish people and Palestinian Arabs should divide up the land into two states. Then in 1948, the State of Israel was established. This was not the end of the story. Israelis and Palestinians are fighting over land to this day.

Apartheid

1948–94

In 1948, the white-controlled National Party gained power in South Africa. They started enforcing racial segregation—nonwhite South Africans (most of the population) had to live in areas separate from whites and use separate facilities, and interracial marriage was banned. Nelson Mandela, a member of the African National Congress, an anti-apartheid political party, became a protest leader and landed in jail for nearly three decades. International pressure eventually forced the National Party to step down, and Mandela became the first black president of South Africa. A reported 21,000 people died during apartheid.

Korean War

1950–53

Before WWII, North and South Korea were one big Korea that had been annexed and occupied by Japan. Then after Japan's WWII loss, Korea was up for grabs. The North was supported by the Soviets and the South was supported by the US. Then in 1950, the North (with Soviet backing) decided to fly south, or invade the territory supported by the US. Hello, Cold War. This is thought of as its first military action. No one won. Fast-forward to today and NK and SK are still quite literally divided.

Vietnam War

1955–75

During and after WWII, a communist movement—led by a guy named Ho Chi Minh—arose in Vietnam in response to international powers (namely Japan and France) trying to control the country. The Soviets supported Ho and his communists in the North and the US supported the non-communist leader in the South. Sound familiar? After decades of fighting and more than one million lives lost, the communists won out.

Thing to know
Viet Cong. The nickname used for Ho Chi Minh's military, short for "Vietnamese Communist." And the nickname has a nickname—it's often shortened to just VC.

Suez Crisis

1956

The one in season two of *The Crown*. Back then, a company run by Britain and France owned the Suez Canal in Egypt, an important trade route. But a new Egyptian leader—who had cozied up to the Soviet Union—decided to say *mine* to the canal. He nationalized it, with the support of the Soviets. Cue Britain, France, and Israel invading and taking back the canal. The US was not happy with its allies' moves, as it feared Soviet retribution and a costly conflict. It threatened economic sanctions against the three countries if they didn't withdraw. The threats did the trick, and Egypt came out a winner. This marked a decline in British and French influence in the Middle East and a signal that colonialism was becoming a thing of the past.

Sputnik

1957

The first satellite launched into space. By the Soviets. Important, since it's considered the start of the space race. Space race: the part of the Cold War where the US and Soviets had a "Whose rocket is bigger?" contest. Sputnik made it clear that the Americans weren't measuring up, and kicked the US space program into high gear.

Bay of Pigs

1961

In 1959, Fidel Castro took over Cuba. And the US immediately started sweating. Castro was a communist and set on decreasing American influence in the country. When he traded friendship bracelets with the Soviet Union, the US said, "We need to get rid of him." So they invaded. The main entry point was an area called, yup, the Bay of Pigs. The US badly underestimated the strength of the Cuban forces and ended up retreating.

Cuban Missile Crisis

1962

The sequel to the Bay of Pigs. The US discovered that the Soviets were stashing secret missiles in Cuba. Not good, since Cuba is 90 miles from Florida. In a post–Bay of Pigs world, the Soviets wanted to deter the US from invading Cuba again. And the US wanted to avoid a nuclear war. So they quarantined Cuba, blocking Soviet ships from sending anything to the island. After 12 days of nail biting, Russian leader Nikita Khrushchev called JFK and said, *we'll get rid of the missiles if you promise to stay away.* Standoff, off. Cold War, still on.

March on Washington

1963

The mass protest in DC where Martin Luther King Jr. gave his "I Have a Dream" speech. 250,000 people showed up at the Lincoln Memorial for this landmark event of the civil rights movement. They were protesting racial discrimination and supporting the Civil Rights Act, which was at a standstill in Congress. The event served as a global symbol of civil rights and other, smaller marches took place around the world.

Iran Hostage Crisis

1979–81

In 1979, Iran's US-supported government (yes, this was a thing) was toppled and replaced by an Islamic gov who wanted nothing to do with the US. When it came to the Cold War, Iran was on Team Soviet. But mostly because they were anti–US. Shortly after the new gov was put in place, a group of Iranian students stormed the US Embassy in Tehran. They took more than 60 people hostage and held more than 50 of them. For more than a year.

Soviet-Afghan War

1979–1989

In the late '70s, a communist gov came to power in Afghanistan. The largely Muslim population there was opposed to their new leaders and Islamic groups (known collectively as the Mujahideen) began rising up. The Soviet Union stepped in to support the communist gov. So in keeping with the Cold War spirit, the US started supporting the anti-communist Mujahideen. After almost 10 years of violence, the Soviets withdrew and the communist gov fell. But for the US, this victory is much more complicated through a historical lens . . . because it went on to help give rise to Islamic extremist groups like the Taliban and al-Qaeda.

Iran-Contra

1985–86

That time the US secretly and illegally sold arms to Iran to secure a hostage release. And to fund an anti-communist group in Nicaragua. Stick with us. The US wanted to fund the Contras, a Nicaraguan group that was rising up against the new communist gov there. But it couldn't legally do this. The US used the cash money from arms sales to Iran to fund the Contras. Bad look for then US president Ronald Reagan. And illegal in more ways than one, since there was an arms embargo on Iran.

Chernobyl

1986

A Soviet nuclear reactor in Chernobyl, Ukraine (then part of the Soviet Union) exploded during a systems test. It was the worst nuclear accident in history. It's estimated that radiation could eventually cause up to 4,000 deaths. They are seen as casualties of the Cold War, since the Soviets were building up reactors so quickly to compete with the US.

Fall of the Berlin Wall

1989

The end of the Cold War. And the end of the Soviet Union. It was when communist East Berlin said that its citizens were free to cross over into the democratic West and ignore the wall that separated them. This came after years of Soviet leader Mikhail Gorbachev slowly opening up to the West more, to revive the Soviet Union's sluggish economy.

Tiananmen Square massacre

1989

Pro-democracy protests in China did not sit well with its communist gov. More than one million Chinese citizens came out to say *we want things to change around here,* and protested for weeks. Then one day, the Chinese gov responded by arresting and killing them. It's estimated that at least 300 people died in the massacre.

Gulf War

1990–91

Iraq—led by Saddam Hussein at the time—invaded its neighbor Kuwait to try to say *mine* to the country's oil and expand its power in the region. This didn't sit well with the international community. The US and its allies invaded (code name: Operation Desert Storm) and eventually made the Iraqis agree to a peace deal. In it, Iraq agreed to destroy its weapons of mass destruction— aka nuclear, biological, and chemical weapons. To be continued . . .

Rwandan Genocide

1994

After WWI, Rwanda was ruled by Belgium. And Belgium created a class system where an ethnic group called the Tutsis was favored over an ethnic group called the Hutus. The Hutus were the majority in Rwanda, so this caused decades of resentment, even after Rwanda was no longer under Belgian rule. In the 1990s, Hutus murdered as many as 800,000 Tutsis over a 100-day period.

Iraq War

2003–11

The sequel to the Gulf War. After the 9/11 attacks, the Bush administration said it believed that Iraq supported al-Qaeda (the terror group behind 9/11), and that it believed Iraq still had weapons of mass destruction. After a lot of back-and-forth, the US told Saddam *leave or we'll invade.* He didn't leave. So they invaded along with a coalition of allies. After years of occupation and trying to transition Iraq to a democratic gov, violence continued. Thousands of coalition troops died and hundreds of thousands of citizens died. Controversial, especially since it turned out that Saddam didn't have those weapons to begin with.

Ongoing conflicts aren't listed here. Those are coming later. But first . . . relationships.

Relationships

Now that you have some of the history, it's time to take a look at current alliances, frenemies, and enemies. Here are the big military and political alliances and what you need to know about them.

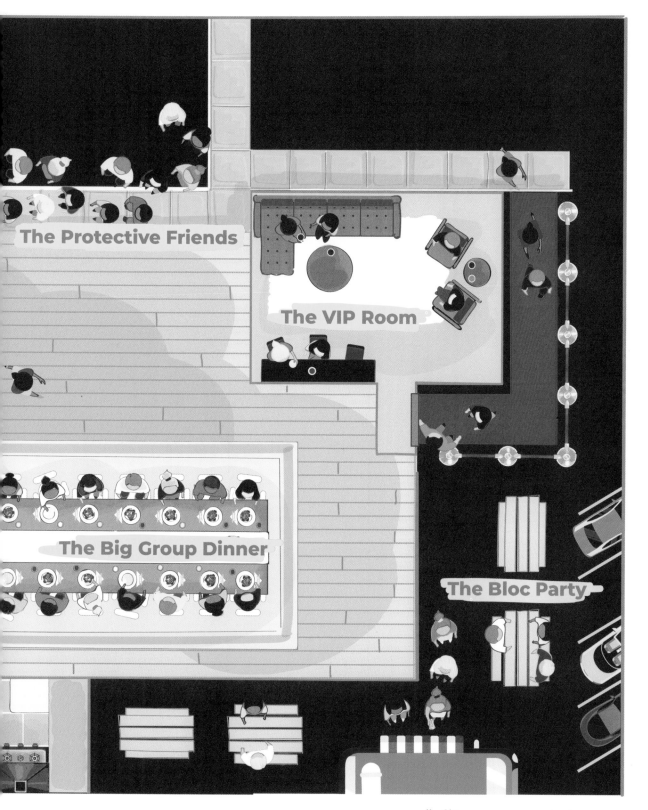

The Protective Friends

The VIP Room

The Big Group Dinner

The Bloc Party

The United Nations: The All-Inclusive Party

The Who

193 countries. So almost everywhere except Palestine and the Holy See. Those two are non-member observer states, meaning they get to attend meetings and use the talking stick but don't get to vote on resolutions.

The What

It was started after WWII, when global leaders had "world peace" on their to-do list more than ever. The UN's charter will tell you that its goal is to maintain international peace and promote human rights. This really means it's a forum for leaders to talk out international issues. And call out countries that aren't playing well with others.

The Where

Every fall, member countries get together at HQ in NYC for the UN General Assembly. This is like the world leaders' Super Bowl. Every country's rep (presidents, prime ministers, and other VIPs) gets to take the floor. They all have the right to create resolutions and vote on them.

The Who's in Charge

The UN Security Council. Because, like in any organization, there are some people who are really running the show.

gang's all here

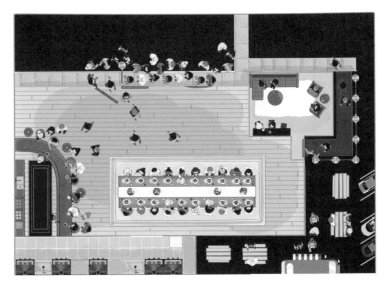

The UN Security Council: The VIP Room

The Who

15 countries. There are five perma members: the US, China, Russia, France, and Britain. Plus 10 temporary members elected for two-year terms by the General Assembly.

The What

The most powerful countries in the world. They also just happen to all have nuclear capabilities. This group alone has the right to impose **sanctions** and authorize peacekeeping operations (that is, deploy military troops to keep the peace in SOS situations). Any one of the permanent members can veto any resolution.

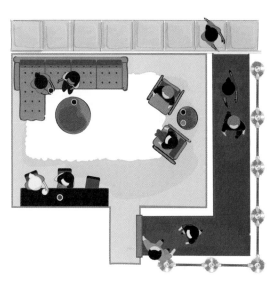

Here's a closer look at them.

United States

The most powerful country in the world. Not only does the US have the number one economy, it spends more on its military than the next seven highest-spending countries combined. So Uncle Sam's the main keeper of international security. And—depending on who you ask—a spreader of democracy or a big ol' meddler.

China

The second largest economy in the world, but experts think it may become number one by 2030. The US and China have gone head-to-head in a trade and technology war in recent years (more on that later). And China's a communist country whose ideas on democracy are pretty much the opposite of the West's.

Russia

The artist formerly known as the Soviet Union. It was once a massive communist superpower in a decades-long standoff with the US, aka the Cold War. Now it's a less massive non-communist superpower causing a lot of US tension. Russia is estimated to have the largest arsenal of nukes in the world. It's also the second largest oil exporter in the world, behind US ally Saudi Arabia. Where Russia throws its support, the US usually throws its opposition. Nyet friends, the two countries almost always play on opposite geopolitical teams.

On the UN Security Council, China and Russia often team up to protect their anti-West agendas. In 2017, they vetoed sanctions on Syria after Syrian president Bashar al-Assad allegedly used chemical weapons on his own citizens. The reason for the veto? Russia supports Assad and is helping him stay in power. China has also vetoed sanctions on North Korea in the past, since it's traditionally supported NK as a buffer for Western influence in the region.

Thing to know
UK vs. Great Britain vs. England. The UK is England, Wales, Scotland, and Northern Ireland. Great Britain is England, Wales, and Scotland. England is just England. England's part of Great Britain, which is part of the UK. If it were high tea time, the UK would be the teapot, Great Britain the water, and England the teabag.

France

Once a major colonial empire, it now has the highest stockpile of nukes in Europe. While France is a major US ally, it's less closely aligned with the US than Britain is. For example, it opposed the Iraq War.

Britain

Formerly the most powerful country in the world, Britain used to have a huge colonial empire. Including, as you know from third-grade history and *Hamilton,* the US. Now, Britain and the US have a "special relationship." The two countries have been close allies during every major twentieth-century conflict. Lately, Britain has dealt with a headache its allies can't help with: Brexit. In 2016, Britain voted to leave the European Union, and they began divorce negotiations.

EU: The Bloc Party

The Who

The European Union. It's made up of 28 member countries. They're neighbors who share a mission statement and, in many cases, a currency (the euro).

The What

On a very practical level, it means that people with passports from EU countries can work and travel freely to other member countries. It's also an economic alliance, meant to stabilize European economies. 19 of the 28 countries in the EU are on the same currency bandwagon. The UK, Sweden, the Czech Republic, Croatia, and Hungary are among the countries that chose to stick with their own currency.

The Why

The EU started as a solution to the nationalism that fueled WWI and WWII. The idea was to bring everyone in the neighborhood to the table to make the rules standardized so it's easier to move goods and people between countries. Make open borders, not war.

The Who's in Charge

The European Commission (EC). It's the EU's executive arm, made up of reps from every EU country. The group makes decisions and enforces legislation for the bloc.

Thing to know
The Czech Republic and Slovakia used to be called **Czechoslovakia.** Add it to the "List of Things You No Longer Say" that includes **"Soviet Union"** and **"the Ukraine."**

Thing to know
Switzerland's right in the middle of the EU, but it flies solo. Because the people there voted to remain independent. The Swiss have a long history of saying "Not it." In WWII, they chose to remain neutral. Which is why people say "I'm Switzerland" when they don't want to get involved.

new kids on the bloc

G7: The Wolf Pack

The Who

The seven best friends that anyone could have. The US, Canada, France, Germany, Italy, Japan, and the UK are all-in.

The What

Coordinating economic, security, and energy policy. Since these seven countries are all wealthy, industrialized democracies, they hold a lot of cards. They're also close allies. And they're not afraid to say "You can't sit with us" when someone's out of line.

The Who's Not Invited

The G7 used to be the G8. In 2014, Russia got the boot from the group after its meddling in Ukraine. More on this later. This put Russia in the international penalty box and turned 8 into 7.

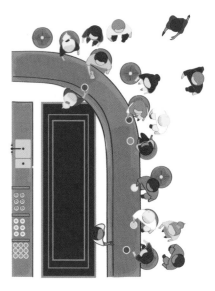

G20: The Big Group Dinner

The Who

Finance ministers and central bank governors from the world's 20 largest economies go. That includes the G7 plus China, Russia, Turkey, Saudi Arabia, Australia, India, and others.

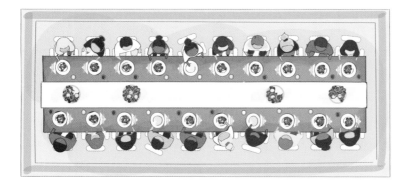

The What

It's the one where everyone talks about the bill. The G20 is basically a less exclusive version of the G7, with a more exclusive focus on the economy. Together, these countries make up more than 80 percent of the world's economy and two-thirds of the world's population. They meet once a year to talk about everything from trade to financial markets and the growth of emerging economies.

NATO: The Protective Friends

The Who

29 mainly European countries plus the US and Canada.

The What

The North Atlantic Treaty Organization. A political and military alliance. An attack on any one member country would be treated as an attack on all of the members.

The Why

To have one another's backs. The group got together at the start of the Cold War to stand up against threats from the then Soviet Union. Today, Russia really isn't into the fact that NATO has added members on its borders (including Estonia, Latvia, and Lithuania).

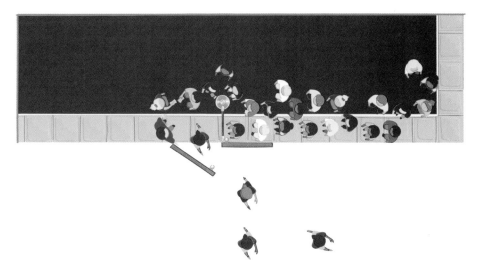

Acronyms FTW

There are also groups and orgs that focus on more specific topics. Here are some of them.

For when your friend won't Venmo you back . . .

The IMF wouldn't stand for this. The **IMF,** or International Monetary Fund, is made up of 189 countries. So almost every country in the world is in on the fun(d). The goal? To help countries keep currency values on the upswing and help them restructure their debt. And avoid another Great Depression. While the G20 is also focused on the economy, the IMF is more all encompassing.

For when gas prices are down . . .

Thank OPEC. **OPEC,** or the Organization of the Petroleum Exporting Countries, is made up of 14 countries that produce half of the world's crude oil. It focuses on keeping oil prices stable by working together on things like how much oil they should produce at once. When you see gas prices going up, you can usually blame OPEC. When you see gas prices going down, you can usually thank OPEC. As the world's largest oil exporter, Saudi Arabia is the boss of the group.

For when you're overdue for a doctor's visit . . .

WHO needs health? Everyone. WHO stands for the World Health Organization. It works with pretty much every country in the world—plus the UN, other international orgs, foundations, and research groups—to make sure people are living a healthy life. Think: making sure people have clean air and water, and helping people fight off diseases like Ebola, HIV, and cancer by giving them access to treatments.

For when your friends are talking about a sports trade . . .

Let's talk international trade. The **WTO,** or World Trade Organization, is—spoiler— the world's trading organization. Job responsibilities include acting as a safe place for countries to talk trade deals, making sure there's open trade around the globe, and playing middleman for any disputes. *Psst* . . . trade doesn't include only goods. It can also include services and intellectual property. The WTO also acts as a referee. Countries can file suit here if they think another country is cheating on trade deals.

Current Conflicts

There are friends and alliances and acronyms. Then there are frenemies and enemies and ideological battles. Here's a closer look at some major, lasting global conflicts and issues.

The US vs. China

Their economic competition is just the tip of the geopolitical iceberg. Enter: the tech and trade wars between the two countries.

Trade

The two are playing a game of "Anything you can tax I can tax higher." In 2018, the US hit China with tariffs on $34 billion worth of goods. Meaning China has to pay more to send them to the US, and those products are more expensive for American consumers (so less likely to sell). China hit back with its own high tariffs. This back-and-forth hit both economies. Hard.

Tech

They're in a race to dominate **5G**—a new wireless Internet system that would make your smartphone or car connect to the Web really quickly. 5G networks are also expected to be able to do things like steer driverless cars and help docs perform surgeries while OOO. The two countries are spending billions of dollars to try to be first to the 5G market. And China's been accused of stealing valuable ideas (IP, or intellectual property) from the US.

Regional issues

China's been saying *mine* to contested areas of the South China Sea. It's fueled a bitter rivalry between China and its Asian neighbors who also claim the area—the Philippines, Taiwan, Vietnam, and Japan. Insert water fights with no signs of stopping. And concern from the US about an expanding Chinese presence in Asia.

The US vs. Russia

The US has been smiling and shaking Russia's hand in person—and then talking behind its back—since the fall of the Soviet Union in the early 1990s.

Russia misses its big empire from the old Soviet days and looks at the expansion of NATO as a major threat. It also doesn't like that the US has ties to countries on its borders.

In 2014, the relationship turned from bad to worse when Russia decided to support separatists in Ukraine (against the wishes of the US) and back President Assad in the Syrian Civil War (also against the wishes of the US).

Then it came out that Russian hackers had attempted to influence the outcome of the 2016 presidential election in favor of President Trump. Cue an investigation into whether people on Team Trump colluded with Russia. The investigation found no evidence of collusion.

Russia's still a major player in international politics and still has the largest collection of nuclear weapons, so the US is stuck between a vodka bottle and a hard place.

Nationalism vs. Globalism

As the world has become increasingly connected—thanks to everything from the Interwebs to trade deals to immigration—nationalist movements have arisen worldwide in response. Here's how some of them have played out.

The EU

Over the past few years, the EU's been dealing with its worst migrant and refugee crisis since WWII. Millions of people fleeing violence in the Middle East and Africa have come to the EU. Some countries have rolled out the welcome mat. Others have put up do not disturb signs. Politicians and movements have capitalized on this fear of incoming migrants and refugees. Example: One of the reasons the UK voted for Brexit was to secure its borders. And anti-immigrant parties have been gaining steam in France and Germany.

Thing to know
Populism vs. nationalism—
different, but with a lot of
overlap. Populist movements
are about taking a
government back from the
"out-of-touch elites" in charge.
Nationalist movements are
specifically focused on
elevating one's country over
others. In recent years, these
have been similar, since those
"out-of-touch elites" have
largely favored globalism.

The US

Two words—Donald Trump. His 2016 election upset leaned on nationalist rhetoric. His campaign was antiestablishment and focused, in part, on a much stricter immigration policy. It also exposed deep divisions within the country.

Islamic Extremism vs. the West

To start, Islam is not the same as Islamic extremism. Islamic extremists are radical groups that oppose tolerance of different faiths, individual liberty, and democracy. Which is why many Islamic extremist groups are against the West.

In 2014, ISIS—an offshoot of al-Qaeda—gained momentum in Iraq and Syria. Its goal? To create a caliphate, or worldwide fundamentalist Muslim state. It's estimated that more than 1,200 people outside of Iraq and Syria have been killed by attacks inspired or planned by ISIS.

The West has put a lot of money toward fighting back against the rise of Islamic extremist groups. The US alone has spent nearly $3 trillion on counterterrorism efforts since 9/11.

Saudi Arabia vs. Iran

This rivalry goes *wayyy* back. That's because they're part of different Islamic sects (**Shiite and Sunni**) that haven't gotten along for centuries. While their rivalry started with ideological differences, now they battle for dominance in the Middle East. Iran is largely Shiite, and Saudi Arabia is largely Sunni.

The two countries have taken this rivalry out in numerous proxy wars. Since 2015, the civil war in Yemen has been fought between Houthi rebels (backed by Iran) and the Yemeni gov (backed by Saudi Arabia).

In the Syrian Civil War, Iran's been supporting the Shiite-led government for years, while Saudi Arabia supports the rebels trying to give the gov the boot.

The US traditionally has a good relationship with Saudi Arabia, thanks to a mix of oil (it has a ton of it), money (it invests in the US economy), and defense (it helps keep relative stability in the region). And Iran is an enemy thanks to ideological differences (Iran has said it wants to "destroy" US ally Israel) and its commitment to nuclear development.

Israelis vs. Palestinians

The Israeli-Palestinian conflict is one of the most divisive in the world. A lot of it goes back to land and security. Specifically, who owns it and how it's controlled.

Right before WWII, the land that is now Israel used to be part of British-controlled Palestine. Right after WWII, the UN said that the Jewish people and Palestinian Arabs should divide up the land into two states. Soon after, the State of Israel was established.

Both sides claim parts of the same land, including the city of Jerusalem as their capital. The ongoing conflict's killed thousands, left millions of Palestinian refugees living in camps in places like Jordan and Lebanon, and put civilians on both sides through ongoing violence.

Some say this is about having a homeland for the Jewish people where they feel secure. Others say this is about Palestinians having had their homeland and security taken away from them. See the problem?

Despite numerous attempts at peace deals and two-state solutions, there is still no peace.

Iran vs. the US

The two countries have had no formal relations since 1980.

Iran is ruled by an Islamic gov that's vowed the "destruction" of US ally Israel and won't even acknowledge it politically. That's part of the reason the West was so concerned by Iran's nuclear development.

In 2015, Iran and the US, plus five other countries, shook on a deal to curb Iran's nuclear enthusiasm in exchange for lifting sanctions on the country.

Then in 2018, President Trump withdrew from the deal, saying it wasn't tough enough on Iran.

Arab Spring

A series of pro-democracy protests that happened in the Middle East and North Africa. Some were successful. Some not so much.

Starting in 2011, these uprisings caught on in Tunisia, Morocco, Syria, Libya, Egypt, and Bahrain.

The result? Regime change in Tunisia, Egypt, and Libya. And a lot of unrest in Syria . . .

Syrian Civil War

In 2011, Syria caught the Arab Spring bug.

Anti-government protests broke out. Syrian President Bashar al-Assad did NOT appreciate these and responded with a massive crackdown.

Soon, this was a full-blown civil war, involving dozens of different groups with different agendas. The problem? Some of these rebel groups were extremist. ISIS was one of them.

Team Moderate Rebels was supported by the US and the West, while Assad's gov has been supported by Russia and Iran.

Assad has been accused of launching chemical weapons attacks on his own people. And more than 500,000 have died in the conflict.

War in Afghanistan

In 2001, about a month after 9/11, the Bush administration went to war with Afghanistan.

The goal? Destroy al-Qaeda (the terror group responsible for 9/11) and the Taliban political group that helped it take root.

Today, the US is still involved in the conflict there. That's because the Taliban is still active, powerful, and fighting the Afghan government (supported by the US) for power. There have been more than 100,000 deaths.

South Sudanese Civil War

Until 2011, South Sudan didn't exist. It got its independence after a nearly 22-year civil war.

But since its independence, the tensions haven't gone away. The dozens of ethnic groups in the country have been fighting for control. And in 2013, a civil war broke out, and fighting has escalated ever since. Some estimates have put the death toll at close to 400,000.

Ukrainian Conflict

Once upon a time, when the Soviet Union was a thing, Ukraine was part of it.

Since then, Ukrainians in the country's East have been nostalgic for the old days, but most would rather strengthen ties with Europe.

In 2013, the Ukrainian president decided to pass on a trade deal with the EU in favor of cozying up to Russia. This didn't sit well with a lot of Ukrainians, and he was eventually ousted.

But Crimea—a pro-Russian peninsula in Ukraine—voted to be part of Russia. Russia welcomed them into the fold. This sparked an uprising from pro-Russian separatists in eastern Ukraine who wanted to join Russia too.

All of this was a big red flag to the US, since it signaled that Russia was expanding its influence in the territory, and fueling violence in Ukraine.

In 2014, the world woke up to just how bad the fighting was when a commercial plane was shot down over Ukraine, killing 298 people. The missile was allegedly fired by a Russian military unit.

Crimea is now part of Russia. File this under "Reasons the US has Russia on its sh*t list."

Venezuelan Crisis

Venezuela's economy was once on the upswing, thanks to its hefty oil supply. But dropping oil prices hit its economy hard.

Now the country has been in crisis mode for years. The currency is basically worthless. There's a shortage of food, water, and other basics. And millions of people have reportedly fled the country, prompting a migrant and refugee crisis in neighboring countries.

Mass protests have called for President Nicolas Maduro and his socialist gov to step down. The US supports the opposition there led by Juan Guaido. Things seem to be getting worse for Maduro—so much so that when you're reading this, he might be out of a job and Guaido could be in charge.

North Korea

Ever since the North and the South were divided in the aftermath of WWII, NK has been an enemy of the West.

So the West is not excited by the fact that NK has been going nuclear. For years, the country's been trying to bulk up its nuclear weapons program—including testing missiles that some say have the capability to hit the US. Breathe.

The country is under strict UN sanctions. Millions are reportedly living in poverty, and the gov reportedly controls everything from where people live to what they do for a living to the haircuts they can get. Really.

Tensions have gotten so bad that even China—who's traditionally supported NK by vetoing UN sanctions against the country—voted to put them in a time-out. The West is hoping that by crippling NK's economy, they'll be able to convince the regime to quit it with the nukes.

theSkimm: The world has billions of people and billions of years under its belt. It's impossible to Skimm all of it. But in order to understand what's happening now, it's important to understand the historical context and underlying powers at play.

Things with an Org Chart

theSkimm on US Government

Overheard everywhere: "Congress can't agree on anything."

"Nothing will get passed." "The government might shut down." The political gridlock you read and hear about all the time might make you want to say "Can't they just get sh*t done already?" There are reasons why it happens. A lot of it traces back to the two-party system. And some of it traces back to the structure of the federal government.

The Org Chart

In some ways, the federal government org chart isn't that different from the one at your company. There are three main departments: the executive, legislative, and judicial branches. There's a CEO: the president. And there's a lot of interoffice drama.

Legislative

How many people are in Congress?

There are 535 people on the congressional group chat. That includes the two chambers: the Senate and the House of Representatives. The Senate has two senators per state. So 100 total. The House has 435 people, distributed in proportion to a state's population. Which is why California has 53 reps and Rhode Island has two.

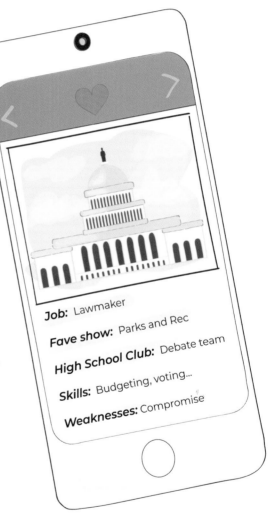

Job: Lawmaker

Fave show: Parks and Rec

High School Club: Debate team

Skills: Budgeting, voting...

Weaknesses: Compromise

What is Congress's role?

To make laws. Which is why its members are called legislators. They also have the power to remove the president from office, confirm or reject a president's cabinet nominations, and declare war. Plus, the power of the purse, or the ability to tax, pass a budget, and decide where money goes.

When does all this actually happen?

In sessions. A **session** in Congress refers to a calendar year, beginning in early January. Every Congress has two sessions in one **term.** Senators are elected for six years (three terms), while representatives serve for two years (one term). So every two years, it's turnover time. Hi, midterm and general elections.

How does Congress get things done?

If you find out, let them know. Here's how two of Congress's biggest responsibilities play out.

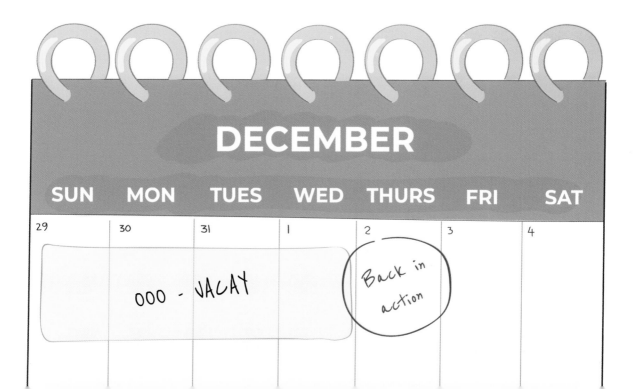

Turning Bills into Laws

While it might seem like Congress can't do its job, there are hundreds of bills passed every year. It's time to brush up on your *School House Rock.*

Thing to know
Authorization bills vs. **appropriation bills.** Authorization bills establish or continue a federal agency or program. Appropriation bills give that agency money.

Idea

This can come from anyone. A rep, senator, organization, or you. Contact your representatives if you have an idea. Really. The more specific your bill, the better chance it has. To contact them, call the Capitol switchboard at 202-224-3121.

Introduction

A senator or rep sponsors a bill, which is given a number. House bills start with "H.R." Senate bills start with "S." The bill's title, sponsors, and co-sponsors (other members who support it) are published in the **Congressional Record**, which is like Congress's blog. If you want to see what Congress has been up to, you can check it out at congress.gov/congressional-record.

Committee

Congress's version of forwarding an email. The bill is sent to the appropriate committee. Committees are smaller groups of legislators who specialize in specific issues. Example: The House Homeland Security Committee gets sent bills about issues like human trafficking and border protection. After they take a red pen to the bill, they send it to a subcommittee for more revision. If people can't agree, the bill dies. If they can, it goes to the House or Senate floor, depending on where it originated. May the odds be ever in its favor.

YES?

NO?

House

The House has limits for how long they can debate a bill.

Thing to know

Hopper. In the House, a bill is introduced by placing it in a box called the hopper. The term comes from the name of bins used to store grain or coal. Ho ho hopper.

Senate

The Senate does not. A **filibuster** is when a senator makes a really, really long speech on the floor to block anything else from getting done. It's the political way of saying *pay attention to me*.

Vote

Members of the House or Senate vote on the bill. If there's a majority in favor, it goes to the other chamber for a yay or nay. That's literal in the Senate. Senators vote by saying "yea" or "nay"; the House votes electronically.

YES?

NO?

The president's turn

The bill is sent to the president for a thumbs-up or a veto.

BILL

signed, sealed, delivered. I'm yours, 'Murica

Passing Budgets

Congress has money on its mind. Since it's responsible for paying the federal bills, it needs to sign off on where money goes. Here are the steps to getting that done.

Wish list

The president submits a budget proposal to Congress. It's pretty much a wish list, but it signals what the prez's top priorities are.

Resolutions

The House and Senate draft budget resolutions. This is their chance to set overall spending levels. Then, the House and Senate budget committees each hold hearings with agency officials, to let them explain why they need that cash money from the gov. The final budget resolution needs to be passed by majority votes in the House and Senate.

Appropriations

The budget resolution is used as a road map to guide appropriation bills. Those bills start in the House and specify funds for each agency in the budget. That includes federal departments like the Department of Health and Human Services, the Department of Defense, and the National Park Service. The final bills go to the floor for a vote.

Signed, sealed, delivered

The president signs or vetoes the budget, like any other bill. With more dollars on the line.

What happens if a budget doesn't pass?

Lights out in D.C. The gov's fiscal year runs from October 1 to September 30 of the following year. Congress has until the end of that year to agree on the bill for the upcoming year. If the deadline's looming and they're still fighting, you start hearing the words *government shutdown.* To avoid playing "Closing Time," Congress can pass a stopgap bill, or a **continuing resolution (CR)**— a short-term spending bill that keeps things running temporarily. In a gov shutdown, only essential agencies (including border protection, in-hospital medical care, power grid maintenance) are allowed to keep going. Others go on **furlough,** which is like a forced vacay. Except it's unpaid.

Thing to know
Omnibus bills. A two-in-one deal. This is when Congress rolls up multiple appropriations bills into one, because they can't complete all the separate bills. It's also a way for legislators to bury controversial provisions into one massive bill. Sneaky, sneaky.

What about the debt ceiling?

Different from the budget. But also something stressing Congress out. The debt ceiling is how much money the US gov can borrow, or how much debt it can go into. If it goes over the debt ceiling, it's like you failing to make a mortgage payment. It can really hurt the US's credit. Yes, countries have credit too.

Thing to know
Budget deficit vs. **debt ceiling.** The budget deficit is how much bigger the gov's spending is than what it's making in any given year. The debt ceiling is how much debt the federal gov's allowed to have.

What are some of the VIP congressional positions?

Speaker of the House

The head of the House of Representatives and arguably the most important position in Congress. On his or her to-do list? Set the House calendar and decide when bills get voted on. Appoint committee heads, influencing how bills are formed and debated. Call the House to order. The Speaker is next in line to the presidency after the vice president.

Majority leader

The spokesperson for the party that has the majority in the chamber. There's one of these in the House and the Senate.

Minority leader

The spokesperson for the party with a minority in the chamber. Also exists in the House and the Senate.

Whip

The Robins to the leaders' Batmans. There's a majority whip and a minority whip. They're the leaders' assistants and the party cops. They take attendance and try to convince senators to vote along party lines.

So you wanna run for Congress?

Impressed. But there are requirements. For the Senate, you have to be 30, a US citizen for at least nine years, and live in the state you rep. For the House, you have to be 25, a US citizen for seven years, and also live in the state you rep. Senators serve for six-year terms while reps serve for two. Good luck.

Executive Branch

More self-explanatory. This one's presidential HQ, or the president and all of his or her people.

What's the role of the executive branch?

To carry out laws. The president's cabinet is made up of the VP plus 15 cabinet members whose job it is to enact and carry out laws in different categories. Here's the breakdown of everyone involved.

President

The CEO of the USA. We don't need to tell you what the president's role represents. But we will remind you that the prez is technically the head of the government and commander in chief of the military. Oh, and that the prez has the power to veto anything passed by Congress. Or **pocket veto,** which is the political version of ghosting. If a president doesn't sign a bill within 10 days, it gets signed. But if Congress goes out of session during those 10 days, it counts as an automatic rejection, aka pocket veto.

VP

The veep is the head of the Senate. The VP is also supposed to stand in for the president at events if he or she doesn't show up. And if the president's impeached or dies, he or she gets the top job.

Cabinet

The president's inner circle. The VP is also included in this crew. Aside from the attorney general, they're all called secretaries. Some of the biggest ones are sec of state, sec of the treasury, sec of homeland security, sec of defense.

Job: Prez

Fave show: West Wing

High School Club: Student Body President

Skills: V popular

Weaknesses: Work/Life balance

Thing to know
Executive order vs. **executive action.** Both are enacted by a president. But an executive order is legally binding, while an executive action is more of a catchall term for something a president wants to get done. Think of them like a signed contract (executive order) vs. a verbal promise (executive action).

So you wanna run for president?

If you're 35, were born in the USA, and have been a resident for at least 14 years . . . go for it.

What's the role of the judicial branch?

To interpret the laws. They are the constitutional translators, and they weigh in on specific cases to decide whether something is legal or not. You hear about the Supreme Court all the time. But in order for a case to make it there, it has to go through a lot of lower courts first.

How many people are on the Supreme Court?

There are nine justices, aka Supremes, on the bench. A president nominates them and the Senate Judiciary Committee conducts hearings and votes whether a nomination should go to the full Senate for confirmation or rejection.

Once appointed, justices serve for their entire lives or until they want to retire.

Job: Justice

Fave show: Law & Order

High School Club: Mock Trial

Skills: Commitment

Weaknesses: Repeat outfit offender

How does the confirmation process work?

For the Supremes, you can't hurry love or confirmation. It's a long process. Here are the steps it takes.

Speed dating

Once someone is nominated, they start speed dating with lawmakers to try to win their vote. This is when senators get some quality one-on-one time to ask the nominee about things like their stance on abortion or healthcare.

Background checks

Meanwhile, the Senate Judiciary Committee starts getting all up in the nominee's business. As in reviewing background checks and taking a hard look at everything from their financial records to past court decisions.

Interview

Next, the nominee goes to Capitol Hill for an intense public job interview, aka confirmation hearing, with the committee. It's on TV, so get some popcorn. Lawmakers get to grill them on their qualifications.

pick me, choose me, love me

V is for vote

After that, the Senate Judiciary Committee votes yea or nay on whether to recommend the nominee for the job. Then the whole Senate gets to weigh in. Most nominees get the job but some don't, because of anything from partisan politics (Merrick Garland in 2016) or supporting white supremacy (Harrold Carswell in 1970). This entire process usually takes two to three months.

> **Thing to know**
> Senators used to need 60 votes to green-light a Supreme. But in 2017, when Justice Neil Gorsuch was going through the process, the GOP voted to change the rules. Now it requires only 51 votes.

What are some of the biggest Supreme Court cases in history?

How much time do you have? The highest court in the land's been judgy since its founding in 1789. Meet (or get reacquainted with) some of the biggest episodes in judicial history.

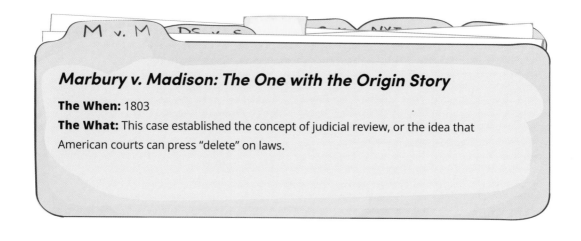

Marbury v. Madison: The One with the Origin Story

The When: 1803
The What: This case established the concept of judicial review, or the idea that American courts can press "delete" on laws.

Dred Scott v. Sandford: The One with the Dreadful History

The When: 1857
The What: This one denied citizenship to African Americans and declared that they could never be US citizens. But in 1868, the Fourteenth Amendment to the Constitution granted citizenship to *all* people born in the US.

Brown v. Board of Education: The One with the Desegregation

The When: 1954
The What: This one desegregated schools. Before this, states were allowed to make their own rules, and many southern states chose to segregate. This ruling made that illegal.

New York Times v. Sullivan: The One with the Headlines

The When: 1964

The What: This set the standard for libel. It made it so that someone suing for libel had to prove actual malice, or that the story was intentionally false or harmful.

Loving v. Virginia: The One for Lovers

The When: 1967

The What: This struck down state laws banning interracial marriage.

Roe v. Wade: The One with the Controversy That Never Ends

The When: 1973

The What: This made abortions federally legal within a woman's first two trimesters. If it were overturned, the decision would be up to states.

US v. Mo

United States v. Morrison: The One About Violence Against Women

The When: 2000

The What: This declared parts of the Violence Against Women Act unconstitutional. The act was passed to give survivors of violence more resources—including money toward investigating and prosecuting their cases. But then the Supremes ruled that part of it (the part that let women sue their alleged attackers in federal court) counted as Congressional overreach. Many considered this a setback for women's rights.

DoC v. H

District of Columbia v. Heller: The One with Guns Blazing

The When: 2008

The What: This clarified that all citizens have a right to keep guns at home for self-defense. Before this, keeping a gun at home was illegal in D.C.

CU v. FEC

Citizens United v. Federal Election Commission: The One with Deep Pockets

The When: 2010

The What: This made election season more flush by ruling that corporations and unions can spend unlimited amounts on campaigns.

Burwell v. Hobby Lobby Stores: The One with the Religious Rights

The When: 2014

The What: This one decided that corporations with religious owners aren't required to pay for contraception coverage.

Obergefell vs. Hodges: The One with the Rainbows

The When: 2015

The What: This one legalized gay marriage in all fifty states. Love actually is all around.

theSkimm: In order to actually understand today's political news, it's important to know how stuff works. This is how it works.

Things That
Effect Change*

theSkimm on Civic Engagement

Even if you don't live on Capitol Hill or aspire to run for office, there's an easy way to effect change in your community and the world: voting.

There are no excuses not to do it. theSkimm is all about getting people registered and committed to show up at the polls.

Here's a look at everything you need to know about elections: how to get registered and vote, the different types of elections, the process from primary to general, and the controversies surrounding election season. Plus, some of the major issues that shape a candidate's platform.

*It really is effect, not affect in this case. We were shocked too.

Why do I need to vote?

Because if you're eligible to, it's your responsibility. Because it's a privilege and a way to effect real change. You're electing the people who make decisions about your life— everything from your healthcare to your taxes to who has access to guns. Despite all this, Americans have a history of low turnout.

Why is turnout so low?

Depends on whom you ask. Some people can't vote because of controversial voter ID laws. More on those later. But for the majority of Americans, it's low because of excuses, or because people don't believe their vote actually matters. Spoiler: It does. More than 100 million Americans headed to the polls in 2018, making it tied for the largest turnout for a midterm election in more than 100 years. Progress. But still, less than half of Americans vote.

OK, I get it. Remind me how to vote.

Get registered.
It takes an average of two minutes or less and you can get it done at theskimm.com/noexcuses. *Psst* . . . don't remember whether you're registered? We've got you covered there too.

Find your polling station.
Once you're registered, you can easily find this online with your address and zip code.

Get prepped.
About two-thirds of states require you to bring some form of ID to the polls. About half of states require a photo ID. That includes driver's licenses, state-issued ID cards, military ID cards, and passports. Make sure to check what your state requires.

Get to the polls.
Do it to it.

What if I can't vote in person?

There are absentee ballots for that. The state you're registered to vote in will mail you a ballot. You fill it out. And send it back. Easy. Every state offers an absentee ballot, but they all have different rules around it. Here are some of them.

Tell us why

Some states require you to tell them why you can't show up on Election Day.

In-person absentee

Some states let you apply for, fill out, and submit your absentee ballot in person before Election Day.

Permanent absentee

Some states will automatically send you an absentee ballot for all future elections. Meaning: You don't need to apply for one after the first time.

All-mail

Some states mail every registered voter a ballot before Election Day. And you can either send it back in the mail or submit it in person.

my dog ate my ballot

What's a valid excuse for a state that requires one?

Every state has different rules for valid excuses, but here are some examples:

For when you still have homework...

If you're a student going to college out of state. Study abroad counts too.

For when you're packing a bag . . .

If you're traveling. Your OOO gives you an excuse to be MIA.

For when you look like the green emoji . . .

If you're sick, injured, or have a disability that prevents you from getting to your polling place.

For when you're serving your country...

If you're a military member, a military member's spouse, or living with some other family member stationed outside your voting location.

My address/name has changed. Do I need to reregister/update my info?

Yes. This process can vary depending on where you live. So double-check. If your state says to submit a new voter registration, you can do that through the US gov's website (USA.gov) or theSkimm's No Excuses website. Click "No" when it asks if you're registered to vote. You'll be prompted to fill out a new registration.

 https://www.theSkimm.com/NoExcuses ➡

How do I switch political parties?

Resubmit your voter registration. Heads-up that in general elections, you can vote for whichever candidates you want, regardless of which party you registered with. It can vary by state, but if you want to be able to vote for a certain party's candidates the next time there are primary elections, you should reregister.

Can I register without a driver's license?

Yes, although you'll still have to provide some sort of ID, like a state ID number or your birth certificate.

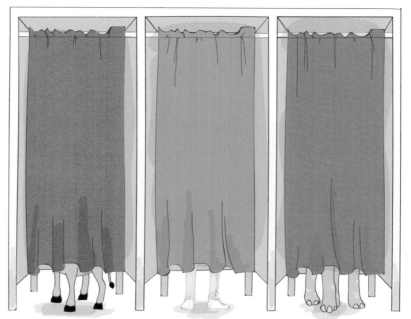

Types of Elections

Primaries. General elections. Midterms. Presidential elections. All big deals, all different things.

Primary vs. General

What is a primary?

The semifinals. It's when America decides which candidates from each major party will go head-to-head in the general election. In a **primary,** you can vote only for candidates in your party. And if you're registered independent, you may not be able to vote in a primary, depending on which state you live in. The dates vary by state, so make sure to check yours at USA.gov. Both midterms and presidential elections have primaries and general election phases. **Super Tuesday** refers to the day in a presidential election where multiple states hold primaries.

What is a general election?

The finals. It's when you select the winner. Unlike primaries, you can vote for whomever you want, regardless of how you're registered. The date is also the same for everyone: the first Tuesday after the first Monday in November.

Midterm vs. Presidential

What is a midterm?

The congressional elections that happen halfway through a presidential term. So they're right in the middle. Every seat in the House of Representatives is up for grabs during midterms. While you don't actually elect a president during midterms, they're considered a temp check on the presidency. They also affect the US's CEO in tangible ways—a midterm can flip the House or Senate, potentially making it difficult for a prez to accomplish his or her goals. One of the biggest differences between a **midterm** and a presidential election (aside from whom you're electing) is the way votes are tallied. In a midterm, whoever gets the most votes in a given state gets the job. Easy. The presidential election voting process gets a lot more complicated. Enter: the **electoral college.**

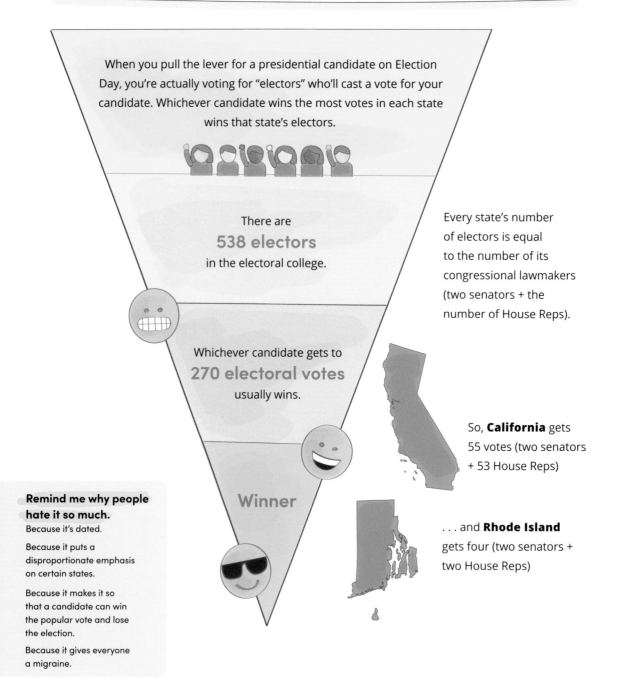

How does the electoral college work exactly?

When you pull the lever for a presidential candidate on Election Day, you're actually voting for "electors" who'll cast a vote for your candidate. Whichever candidate wins the most votes in each state wins that state's electors.

There are
538 electors
in the electoral college.

Whichever candidate gets to
270 electoral votes
usually wins.

Winner

Every state's number of electors is equal to the number of its congressional lawmakers (two senators + the number of House Reps).

So, **California** gets 55 votes (two senators + 53 House Reps)

. . . and **Rhode Island** gets four (two senators + two House Reps)

Remind me why people hate it so much.

Because it's dated.

Because it puts a disproportionate emphasis on certain states.

Because it makes it so that a candidate can win the popular vote and lose the election.

Because it gives everyone a migraine.

How can you win the popular vote and lose the election?

A candidate who receives a state's popular vote gets all of its electors. So it's possible to get more votes overall, concentrated in fewer states, and lose out. This has happened five times in history. Three of them happened in the 19th century. Two of them you probably lived through: George W. Bush's win over Al Gore in 2000 and Donald Trump's win over Hillary Clinton in 2016.

Campaign Finance

Elections are quite a production. Who pays for all this?

Lots of people. Remember that *Citizens United* Supreme Court case? It made it so that campaign contributions count as free speech. So now organizations—like unions and corporations—can spend as much as they want on a candidate. A single individual can contribute up to $2,800 per candidate. *Citizens United* was controversial because money talks—and some get worried it gives too much influence to wealthy people and companies. There are two main ways people contribute to a candidate.

PAC

Through a **political action committee,** which can give money directly to candidates and political parties. But there are rules. PACs are allowed to give only $5,000 per candidate and $15,000 per party in an election.

Super PAC

This is the *Westworld* version of a PAC. It's a choose-your-own-adventure, spend-as-much-as-you-want situation. **Super PACs** can't do things like pay for candidates' private jets, hotel rooms, or anything directly contributing to the campaign. But TV ads are fair game, and they can spend unlimited cash on advertisements supporting their candidates . . . and hating on opponents. They do need to disclose their donors, which is why a lot of people and groups prefer to go dark.

What do you mean *dark*?

Dark money. People and groups that don't want the rest of the world to know what they're spending on elections can donate to certain kinds of nonprofits that don't have to disclose their donors. These are organizations that have gotten the OK from the IRS to give cash to "social-welfare" causes like gun control or protecting the environment. They can also foot the bill for ads supporting candidates who are into their causes.

Dark money and campaign funding aren't the only controversial topics when it comes to the election process. There are a lot of opinions about the rules around voting: how districts are drawn and what people are required to bring to the polls.

Redistricting

How does redistricting work?

In 2020, the gov will collect a ton of data about the country through the census, which determines things like where schools and hospitals should be built and how many House seats each state gets. Once that's determined, state legislatures or independent commissions are responsible for drawing up the district maps (if Colorado gets seven districts, the state also gets seven House seats).

Why is it controversial?

A lot of times politics is involved to help a certain party keep its votes or get more. This is called partisan **gerrymandering.** And it's becoming a big issue. Until the Supremes declare a sweeping stance on this, state lawmakers will likely continue to take advantage. Meaning: The party in power may have the chance to draw your district maps—which can keep your state leaning red or blue for decades.

How do voter ID laws work?

They vary by state. Some states say "No ID, no problem." Others require you to show some face, literally. That means photo IDs issued by the gov, like driver's licenses and passports. Seven states—Georgia, Indiana, Kansas, Mississippi, Tennessee, Wisconsin, and Virginia—have laws that require a government-issued photo ID.

Why is that controversial?

Because not everyone has a photo ID or can get one easily. It typically costs money to get a government ID, and often costs money to get to the polls. Some in the GOP say strict voter ID laws prevent voter fraud. Dems say not so—they just keep minorities and low-income people from voting.

The Big Recurring Issues

While there are issues inherent to the election process, there are also issues that are important to who you vote for. Here are some of the biggest campaign issues, the opinions, and why a candidate's stance matters.

Gun Control

The background

The Second Amendment was put in the Constitution to give citizens the right to defend themselves and their families. Fast forward more than 200 years later, there are hundreds of mass shootings a year.

The opinions

Everyone agrees that mass shootings need to stop. Not everyone agrees on how to stop them, and who to blame. The recent pushes for reform have focused on things like universal background checks and making a digital record of gun purchases. In 2018, more than 1 million people showed up at the March for Our Lives protests across the country. Meanwhile, the NRA (National Rifle Association) and some on the right say that mental health problems, not gun ownership, are to blame and that their Second Amendment rights are under attack.

The Economy

The background

After the '08 financial crisis, the economy had a long hangover. Interest rates dropped to basically zero to help give the economy a boost by making it easier for people to borrow money. In recent years, interest rates and job numbers have been looking up. How a candidate plans to keep the economy on the rise is a major talking point.

The opinions

Everyone wants to continue boosting employment and creating job growth. But some (mostly on the left) would like to focus on programs like Social Security and Medicare, and closing the wealth gap. Others (mostly on the right) want to focus on supporting big companies to encourage economic growth for everyone.

Climate Change

The background

The Earth's heating up. And as you read earlier in this book, some recent reports have been even worse than expected. A 2018 UN report said the world has 12 years to significantly reduce greenhouse gas emissions . . . or we could start seeing severe impacts of climate change by 2040.

The opinions

97 percent of scientists say it's based on human activity. So the vast majority of experts believe this is a major problem. But there are a lot of political opinions about how major it really is. Some (mostly on the left) say *this is becoming a national security issue we need to deal with stat.* Others (mostly on the right) question whether the human effect has been overstated. And others on the right say *climate change might be bad . . . but losing coal jobs and making businesses pay high prices to cut back on emissions is also bad.*

Abortion

The background

Roe v. Wade gave women the right to have an abortion. Typically, they have until the fetus is considered "viable" outside of the uterus. Many states have put that at around 20 to 24 weeks. But some states have cut down that time period. Mississippi recently passed a bill banning abortions after 15 weeks. A federal court struck it down, but the state is appealing.

The opinions

Where to begin? This is one of the most divisive social issues out there and hits on a lot of nerves—women's rights, religion, access to healthcare. Some believe women have the right to a safe, legal abortion, and that when states limit that access, it unfairly targets low-income women, especially in rural areas, who have limited access to clinics. Others believe in the right to life, or the idea that abortion should be illegal in most or all cases. In some cases, this side believes there should be exceptions if the woman was sexually assaulted or to save the life of the mother.

Immigration

The background

There are millions of undocumented immigrants living in the US. For years, lawmakers have been trying (and failing) to come up with a solution. Since President Trump was elected, he's been trying to roll back **DACA** (an Obama-era program that protects from deportation people who were illegally brought to the US as kids, aka "Dreamers") and enact tough-on-immigration policies that got him elected. That includes cracking down on sanctuary cities (places that protect immigrants from deportation), his zero-tolerance policy that separated kids from their parents at the US-Mexico border, a travel ban that aimed to prevent people from several Muslim-majority countries from coming to the US, and building a big ol' wall on our southern border.

The opinions

Most everyone believes it's not okay to separate immigrant families at the border. And that the immigration system needs a makeover. But some (mostly on the right) think priority number one needs to be increasing national security by protecting our borders. Others (mostly on the left) think priority number one should be creating a path to citizenship for undocumented immigrants—especially those in the DACA program.

theSkimm: Voting is the way to make your voice heard on decisions and issues that affect your life. The same life that you've now Skimm'd.

SKIMM'TIO

açaí: A type of berry found on South American palm trees that's high in antioxidants and other nutrients. (page 38)

acidity: The light, citrusy taste of a wine. (page 7)

ACV: Actual cash value. A type of insurance that covers the current cost of an item, rather than what you bought it for. (page 161)

adjusted gross income: Your gross income minus deductions. (page 114)

appreciating asset: Something like a house whose value (hopefully) increases over time. (page 164)

appropriation bills: Bills that deal with the federal government. (page 204)

APY: Annual percentage yield, or the yearly rate of return of the money in your savings account. Accounts with better interest rates have a higher APY. (page 118)

ARM: Adjustable-rate mortgage. Loans that start with a lower interest rate that adjusts every year depending on the markets. (page 163)

authorization bills: Bills that establish or modify federal agencies. (page 204)

avalanche method: Minimize the interest you pay by taking care of debts with the highest interest rates first. (page 117)

balloon mortgage: A mortgage where a lump sum is paid at the end of the loan period. (page 164)

NARY

bear market: When the market's dipping low. (page 125)

bitters: The fancy thing in your drink, aka flavored extracts concocted by infusing things like herbs, seeds, and berries with alcohol. (page 17)

body: The way a wine feels in your mouth, directly related to how much alcohol is in it. (page 6)

bonds: Loans made to a company or the government, paid back at fixed interest rates. (page 124)

brokerage account: The place to park your investments. (page 122)

budget deficit: How much bigger the gov's spending is than what it's making in any given year. (page 207)

bull market: When the market's on the upswing. (page 125)

cage-free: Eggs that were produced by chickens outside a cage. But there are no space requirements for the chicken's space. (page 61)

capital gains: The profits from the sale of an asset (shares of stock, land, home). You can get taxed on these. (page 140)

cash diet: Budget for the daily amount you want to spend on vacation and put that amount in different envelopes labeled by day. (page 51)

CBD: Oil that comes from the flowers or buds of hemp or marijuana plants but doesn't contain THC (the chemical that gets people high). (page 38)

CD: A certificate of deposit. An account with better rates than a regular savings account, but restrictions on withdrawing for a set period of time (usually a few months up to a few years). (page 118)

chia: Seeds from a South American mint plant that are high in protein and fiber. (page 38)

CLEAR: A pricey airport program that feels like a *Black Mirror* episode. It uses your fingerprint and scans your eyes for identification, allowing you to bypass the boarding pass–ID checkpoint. (page 43)

COBRA: Consolidated Omnibus Budget Reconciliation Act. A federal law that may let you keep your health insurance for a period of time after losing your job. (page 148)

co-insurance: The amount you still have to pay for covered medical services once you hit your deductible. (page 146)

communism: A system of gov where all property and means of production are owned collectively. (page 171)

Congressional Record: Congress's blog, or the place where it records bills it's considering. (page 204)

continuing resolution: The short-term spending bill reached when Congress can't agree on a budget. (page 207)

co-pay: The flat fee you pay for covered medical services. (page 146)

corked: Wine that's contaminated with cork taint, which happens when the natural fungi in a cork interacts with certain chlorides or bleaches used to sanitize corks. Drink at your own risk (don't). (page 8)

credit mix: How many types of credit you have in use. (page 156)

credit utilization: The ratio of how much you owe to how much you're allowed to spend. You want to keep this low. (page 156)

Czechoslovakia: The former Czech Republic and Slovakia. Put this on your "List of Things You No Longer Say." (page 187)

DACA: An Obama-era program that protects from deportation people who were illegally brought to the US as kids, aka "Dreamers." (page 227)

day trading: Buying and selling stocks within the same day before the close of the markets. (page 128)

debt ceiling: How much debt the federal gov's allowed to have. (page 207)

deductible: The amount you have to pay toward your medical costs before your insurance company starts picking up part of the bill. (page 146)

deductions: The way to shave off your taxable income. You can go standard or itemized. (page 136)

democracy: A system of gov for the people, where citizens have the right to vote. (page 170)

depreciating asset: Something like a car whose value decreases over time. (page 164)

Dow Jones Industrial Average: The music charts of the stock market. It lists 30 big-name stocks traded on the NYSE or NASDAQ. (page 127)

electoral college: The controversial process of tallying presidential votes. For most states, it's winner-takes-all—whoever wins the popular vote in the state gets all of that state's electors (equal to its number of congressional reps). (page 221)

ETFs: Exchange-traded funds—a type of fund that's traded on a stock exchange. (page 123)

EU: The European Union. It's made up of 28 European countries. (page 187)

executive action: A directive issued by the president that's not legally binding, and treated more as a verbal promise. (page 209)

executive order: A, yes, order issued by the president that's legally binding. (page 209)

exemptions: Tax discounts you get right off the bat for just being you. (page 136)

fermentation: The process of converting sugar into alcohol. (page 4)

FICO score: One of the main credit scores banks use when determining whether to give you a loan. FICO stands for Fair Isaac Corporation, the company whose software calculates your score. (page 154)

50/30/20 rule: A budgeting method. 50 percent of your paycheck goes to things you need (like rent), 30 percent goes towards things you want (like travel) and 20 percent goes towards savings and paying off debt. (page 115)

filibuster: When a senator makes a really, really long speech on the floor to block anything else from getting done. (page 205)

5-4-3-2-1 rule: Packing hack. Bring one hat, two pairs of shoes, three bottoms, four tops, five pairs of socks and underwear. (page 44)

fixed-rate loan: A loan where you pay the same interest rate every year. (page 163)

5G: A new wireless Internet system that would make your smartphone or car connect to the Web really quickly. China and the US are racing to be first to develop it. (page 192)

flax: Seeds from a flax plant that are high in fiber and omega-3 fatty acids. (page 38)

foreclosure: When the bank takes back your house because you stopped paying your mortgage. (page 161)

4-7-8 breathing technique: A breathing technique the involves inhaling through your nose for four seconds, holding for seven seconds, and breathing out through your mouth for eight seconds. (page 25)

4868: The IRS tax extension form. Procrastinator's delight. (page 135)

401(k): An employer-sponsored retirement savings plan that lets you save and invest a piece of your paycheck before taxes are taken out. (page 119)

free fall position: Sleeping stomach down. (page 27)

free-range: Eggs produced by chickens with access to the outdoors. (page 61)

FSA: Flexible savings account. A type of savings account to help pay for healthcare. With an FSA, there are limited options to roll over unused money. (page 148)

furlough: The forced unpaid vacay "nonessential" federal employees go on when there's a government shutdown. (page 207)

gerrymandering: When a party draws district lines to favor their guy or girl. (page 224)

Global Entry: The airport program that lets you skip the customs line. If you have Global Entry, you also get TSA PreCheck. (page 42)

gross income: How much you make before taxes and other deductions are taken out. (page 114)

G7: A security alliance between the US, Canada, France, Germany, Italy, Japan, and the UK. (page 188)

G20: An economic alliance between the world's twenty largest economies. (page 188)

hanger trick: Turn all your hangers one way. When you wear something, turn its hanger the other way. After six months, you'll know what you actually wear and what you can toss. (page 30)

hard inquiry: A type of credit check that affects your score. Happens when a lender checks specifically to approve a new credit card or a loan. (page 156)

hemp: Seeds from a hemp plant that are high in fatty acids and protein. (page 38)

high-yield savings account: An account where you put more in and get more back. The interest rates are often higher but you often need to invest a certain amount to get one. (page 118)

HMO: A health insurance plan that usually limits insurance to in-network coverage. (page 147)

hopper: The box in the House of Representatives where bills are introduced. (page 205)

HSA: Health savings account. A savings account to help pay for healthcare. With an HSA, the unused money in your account rolls over to the next year. (page 148)

hyaluronic acid: A naturally occurring substance, usually found in serum or creams. Its main purpose is to help the skin retain moisture. (page 35)

IMF: International Monetary Fund. Made up of 189 countries, with the goal to restructure debt and help keep currency values on the upswing. (page 190)

in-network: Doctors and hospital systems your insurance company has deals with (where you generally pay less). (page 144)

IP PIN: Identity protection personal identification number. It's like two-step tax verification to make sure no one's using your Social Security number, protecting you from identity theft. (page 140)

IPO: Initial public offering, or when a company's stock has its coming-out party. This is when the public's invited to buy stock. (page 125)

IRA: Individual retirement account. (page 119)

liability coverage: Insurance coverage that protects you if you're sued. (page 160)

log position: Sleeping on your side with arms and legs straight. (page 27)

majority leader: The spokesperson for the party that has the majority in the chamber. (page 208)

market rates: A benchmark for salary negotiations. It's what people in similar positions are getting paid in your industry. (page 90)

Medicaid: Federal and state insurance coverage for people whose salary is under a certain amount. (page 145)

Medicare: Federal and state insurance coverage for people over sixty-five. (page 145)

Medicare-for-all: A single-payer system where the federal gov foots everyone's healthcare bill. (page 151)

midterm: Congressional elections that happen halfway through a president's term. (page 221)

military roll method: Rolling your clothes instead of folding them to make more space. (page 44)

minority leader: The spokesperson for the party with a minority in the chamber. (page 208)

monarchy: A system of gov with a crown, where authority lies in a single monarch. Today, most monarchies are constitutional ones, which sometimes means the monarch is a figurehead. (page 170)

mutual funds: A fund made up of a group of stocks, bonds, etc., professionally managed by an investment firm. (page 123)

Nadi Shodhana: A yoga breathing technique. Plug your right nostril and inhale through your left. Then plug your left nostril and exhale through your right. *Aaand* repeat. (page 26)

NASDAQ: One of the major stock exchanges, known for hosting tech stocks. (page 126)

NATO: North Atlantic Treaty Organization. A political and military alliance between twenty-nine mostly European countries, plus the US and Canada. (page 189)

net income: Your take-home pay after taxes and other deductions. (page 114)

90-minute blocks: A self-explanatory productivity hack. Work for ninety minutes. Take a break. Repeat. (page 108)

NYSE: One of the major stock exchanges, known for hosting stocks from large, stable companies. (page 126)

oaky: The flavor of a wine that was aged in an oak barrel. (page 7)

oligarchy: A system of gov where a small group of people controls everything. (page 171)

omnibus bill: When Congress rolls up multiple appropriations bills into one. (page 207)

120 rule: An investing rule of thumb. The idea is that 120 minus your age is the percentage of your portfolio you should have in stocks. (page 129)

1-3-5 list: Your to-do list whisperer. Every day, check off one big thing, three medium sized things, and five small things. (page 108)

OPEC: Organization of the Petroleum Exporting Countries. Fourteen countries that produce half of the world's crude oil. (page 190)

open enrollment: The period of time every year when you can sign up for health insurance. (page 145)

out-of-network: Doctors and hospital systems your insurance company doesn't have deals with (where you generally pay more). (page 144)

out-of-pocket max: The most you have to pay for covered health services per year. (page 146)

oxidized: When vino has been exposed to too much oxygen. (page 8)

political action committee: PAC. An organization that can give a limited amount of money directly to a candidate or campaign. (page 223)

paper towel trick: Making your wine colder by wrapping a wet paper towel around it and sticking it in the freezer for a few mins. (page 5)

pocket veto: If Congress goes out of session during the 10 days a president has to sign a bill, it gets automatically rejected. (page 209)

Pomodoro technique: A productivity hack. Work without distractions for a timed 25-minute block. Take a five-minute break. Repeat. After four 25-minute working sessions, take a half-hour break to stay creative and move around. (page 108)

populism: A political movement all about returning power to the people and away from the "out-of-touch elites." (page 171)

PPO: A health insurance plan with both in- and out-of-network options, but generally higher premiums. (page 147)

premium: The monthly amount you pay an insurance company for coverage. (page 144)

primary: The election semifinals when America decides which candidates from each party will go head-to-head in the general election. (page 221)

principal: The amount you borrowed in a loan (and agreed to pay back). (page 163)

recession: A serious drop in economic activity that happens for more than a few months. (page 125)

replacement cost: A type of insurance that covers the amount it would take to replace an item. (page 161)

retinol: A form of vitamin A used to reduce fine lines and increase collagen production. (page 35)

Roth IRA: A type of IRA where you pay taxes up front, but don't get taxed when you withdraw. (page 119)

sanctions: Putting a country in the penalty box (for example, freezing assets, suspending trade) for misbehaving. (page 185)

S&P 500: A well-known stock index that tracks 500 large US companies traded on the NYSE or NASDAQ. (page 127)

serum: A water-based skin product made up of small molecules that can get deep into your skin to deliver nutrients. (page 35)

session: A congressional calendar year. (page 203)

Shiite and Sunni: The different sects of Islam. (page 194)

snowball method: A way to get momentum when paying off loans.

Start by listing out all your debts, smallest to largest. Pay the minimum balance on each one, except the smallest. For that one, dedicate as much cash to it as possible each month until it's repaid. Then put that payment amount toward the second smallest debt until it's paid off, and so on. (page 117)

socialism: Like communism, but workers can earn wages and spend them however they choose. (page 171)

soft inquiry: A type of credit check that doesn't affect your credit score, as when a potential employer does a background check. (page 156)

Soviet Union: USSR, or the massive communist superpower that fell at the end of the Cold War in '91. (page 174)

Speaker of the House: The head of the House of Representatives and arguably the most important position in Congress. (page 208)

starfish position: Sleeping on your back with your arms and legs out. (page 28)

stocks: Investments that represent shares of a company. (page 124)

super PAC: The *Westworld* of PACs. An organization that can give an unlimited amount of money indirectly to a candidate or campaign. (page 223)

Super Tuesday: The day in a presidential election season when multiple states hold primaries. (page 221)

tannin: Compounds found in grape seeds, skins, and stems that leave your mouth feeling dry and kinda like you had dark chocolate or black tea. (page 6)

1040: The IRS form used by taxpayers to file annual income tax returns. (page 134)

TAXES AND CHILL

1099: The IRS side-hustle tax form you get from someone you're contracting for. (page 134)

term: Two congressional sessions. (page 203)

"the Ukraine": The way the Soviet Union used to refer to Ukraine when it was its boss. Put this on your "List of Things You No Longer Say." (page 187)

30-day list: A list of all the things you want to buy during a 30-day, self-imposed ban on shopping. At the end of 30 days, if you still want to buy something on the list, go for it. (page 30)

thread count: The number of horizontal and vertical threads per square inch on sheets. Higher isn't always better—anything above 800 is probably BS and a marketing tactic. (page 27)

toner: A liquid skin product that helps get skin's pH balance in check. (page 35)

TSA PreCheck: The most popular way to cut the line at the airport. You don't even have to remove your shoes, laptops, belts, etc. It's also the cheapest option at $85 for a five-year membership. (page 42)

12-12-12 challenge: When cleaning, find 12 things to throw away, 12 to donate, and 12 to put back in their place. (page 30)

UN: United Nations. The alliance of 193 countries (pretty much everyone) that's meant to promote human rights and talk out international issues. (page 184)

UN Security Council: The most powerful countries in the UN and the world. The US, China, Russia, UK, and France are on it. (page 185)

variety and varietal: Variety is a noun that refers to the grape used to make the wine, while varietal is an adjective that describes the wine made using grape varieties. (page 7)

VAT: Value-added tax. The EU tax that makes goods pricier. You can sometimes get a refund on this tax. (page 50)

W-4: The IRS form you fill out when you start a new job, so your employer knows how much to withhold from your paycheck for taxes. (page 133)

W-4 the win

whip: The congressional leaders' assistants and party cops. They take attendance and try to maintain voting along party lines. (page 208)

WHO: World Health Organization. The one that works to make sure global populations are healthy (think: making sure people have clean air and water, fighting diseases, and providing access to medication). (page 191)

WTO: World Trade Organization. An org with the goal of promoting open trade and playing referee for trade disputes. (page 191)

W-2: The sequel to the W-4. It's the IRS form that shows how much of your paycheck was withheld that year. (page 133)

Resources

Capitol Switchboard
1-202-224-3121

Crisis Text Line
text 741741

Health Resources and Services Administration
hrsa.gov

Health insurance
HealthCare.gov

National Alliance on Mental Illness
nami.org

National Suicide Prevention Lifeline
1-800-273-8255

Register to vote
theSkimm.com/noexcuses or USA.gov

Recycling electronics waste
eiae.org

Reporting IRS scams
1-800-829-1040 or email phishing@irs.gov

Acknowledgments

How to Skimm Your Life represents the hard work, passion, and dedication of theSkimm's team and community over the past seven years. A huge thanks to Skimm HQ—this book is a representation of our values as a company and every one of you was involved in bringing it to life. A special thank-you to the dedicated power group who made this happen: Avery Carpenter, Michael Gray, Kaitlyn Jankowski, and Jessica Pepper. This is a physical reminder that we get sh*t done because of how our team hustles and shows up every day. Thank you for starting the year with a Book-a-thon and for embracing the constant stream of ideas that have brought this book to life.

Cheers to our Skimm Squad and Skimm'bassadors—the community who helped spread the word. The mission of this company and this book doesn't exist without you.

To our families—thank you for your constant love, support, and patience. We know we are constantly late, tired, and hungry, and we thank you for your putting up with us. We love you.

Thank you to Sara Weiss for championing our vision for this book, and Gina Centrello, Kara Welsh, Kim Hovey, Jennifer Hershey, Susan Corcoran, Jennifer Garza, Emily Isayeff, Leigh Marchant, Quinne Rogers, Mark Maguire, Simon Sullivan, Nancy Delia, Joe Perez, and the team at Ballantine for their help in bringing this book to theSkimm community.

Thank you to Sarah Rothman and Meredith O'Sullivan Wasson for being our wise counselors, and the team at The Lede Company, especially Anna Bailer, for their support.

Thank you to Esther Newberg, Heather Karpas, and Kristyn Benton at ICM for taking a chance on theSkimm's first book.

Thank you to Kate Childs and Cait Hoyt at CAA for taking our crazy ideas and making them come to life on the road. We cannot thank you enough for the creativity you bring and the way you jumped in with theSkimm team.

theSkimm is made possible by our amazing group of investors who have signed up to be on this crazy journey with us. We could not do this without you. Literally.

Irving Azoff	Gordy Crawford	Meredith Levien	Shonda Rhimes
Tyra Banks	Doug DeMartin	Joe Marchese	Linnea Roberts
Willow Bay	Jesse Draper	Liz Milonopoulos	Jim Robinson
Aimee Beatty	Rich Greenfield	James Murdoch	M. G. Siegler
John F. Blackburn	Chelsea Handler	Matt Newberger	Scott Stanford
Sara Blakely	Mariska Hargitay	Satya Patel	Hope Taitz
Yannick Bolloré	Michael Karsch	Alan Patricof	Lizzie and Jonathan Tisch
Kate Brennan	Michael Kassan	Bob Pittman	
Troy Carter	Nancy and Jeffrey B. Lane	Kim Posnett	John Waldron
Nicole Cook		John Reese	Hunter Walk

theSkimm is constantly supported and challenged by our group of advisors, 911 calls, and people who have been our champions since the couch days.

Linda Boff	Hildy Kuryk	Michelle Peluso	Krista Smith
Fiona Carter	Kristin Lemkau	Laurie Racine	Jon Steinberg
Greg Clayman	Catherine Levene	Dan Rosensweig	Alex Taub
Jenny Fleiss	Christie Marchese	Jane Rosenthal	Alexa von Tobel
Lisa Gersh	Jenny Meyer	Kelly Sawyer	Allison Williams
Desiree Gruber	Betsy Morgan	Dan Schulman	
Jenn Hyman	Misha Nonoo	Judy Smith	

We also want to acknowledge some of the authors who have been part of Skimm Reads, including Megan Abbott, Yrsa Daley-Ward, Stephanie Danler, Emily Giffin, Jessica Knoll, Kevin Kwan, Amy O'Dell, Allison Pataki, Busy Philipps, Taylor Jenkins Reid, Karin Slaughter, Gabrielle Union, Jennifer Weiner, Lauren Weisberger, and Tara Westover.

And finally, we would like to extend our sincere gratitude to our community of Skimm'rs. The company started out as two people on couch. It's grown to what it is today because of your support, trust, and commitment to our mission.

To the people who have gotten up early to attend a Power Breakfast, to those who organized Sip 'n Skimms during an election in their hometowns, to the ones who have asked questions in our AMA's, participated in our No Excuses and Skimm Squads, competed to wear Skimm swag, and wrote us emails with the ideas for their own next step . . . this book is for you.

Thank you.

About theSkimm

theSkimm is a membership company dedicated to helping female millennials live smarter lives. By seamlessly integrating into their existing routines, theSkimm has become a trusted source for more than seven million subscribers.

Founded in 2012 by Carly Zakin and Danielle Weisberg, theSkimm is committed to helping its members through decision-making moments by giving them the information they need to make informed and empowered choices.

theSkimm's flagship product, the Daily Skimm, is the fastest growing newsletter on the market, and the company's product suite has grown to engage with members at home, work, and on-the-go.

theSkimm is time well spent.

Published in the United States by Ballantine Books,
an imprint of Random House, a division of Penguin Random House LLC, New York.

BALLANTINE and the HOUSE colophon are registered trademarks
of Penguin Random House LLC.

LIBRARY OF CONGRESS CATALOGING-IN-PUBLICATION DATA
Names: Skimm, Inc., issuing body.
Title: How to Skimm your life / The Skimm, Inc.
Description: New York: Ballantine Books, [2019]
Identifiers: LCCN 2019003777 | ISBN 9781984820808 (hardcover) |
ISBN 9781984820815 (ebook)
Subjects: LCSH: Women—Life skills guides.
Classification: LCC HQ1221 .H79 2019 | DDC 305.4—dc23
LC record available at https://lccn.loc.gov/2019003777

Printed in the United States of America on acid-free paper

randomhousebooks.com

987654321

First Edition

Designed by theSkimm